VEGAN SOUL FOOD COOKBOOK

VEGAN
Soul Food
COOKBOOK

**Plant-Based, No-Fuss
Southern Favorites**

NADIRA JENKINS-EL

PHOTOGRAPHY BY HÉLÈNE DUJARDIN

callisto
publishing
an imprint of Sourcebooks

Copyright © 2020 by Callisto Publishing LLC

Cover and internal design © 2020 by Callisto Publishing LLC

Photography: © 2020 Hélène Dujardin. Food styling by Anna Hampton.

Author Photo: © 2020 Chris Picciuolo.

Butternut Squash Mac 'n' "Cheese," page 61, and Cajun Fried "Chicken," page 90.

Interior and Cover Designer: Julie Gueraseva

Art Producer: Janice Ackerman

Editor: Myryah Irby

Production Editor: Nora Milman

Published by Callisto Publishing LLC C/O Sourcebooks LLC

P.O. Box 4410, Naperville, Illinois 60567-4410

(630) 961-3900

callistopublishing.com

Printed and bound in China

OGP 2

For my mom and dad for passing on compassion and love for all beings and for my nana for sharing her passion of wanting to feed the world love served on a plate.

Contents

Introduction

Soul food is and has always been a huge part of my life. As a child, I was surrounded by amazing cooks like my father, my mother, and my nana. Cooking brought my family together for any and all occasions.

My nana was the soul food queen on her block in West Philadelphia. When my sister and I would visit her during summers or holidays, our Saturdays were often spent chopping and mixing in preparation for Nana's famous soul food Sunday dinners. I couldn't wait to fix my small tasting bowls as we put the dishes together.

At home, we were mostly vegetarian and ate a more natural, whole foods diet that excluded sugar. My parents were Moorish American, which is a part of Islam, so pork, red meat (which is allowed if kosher, but my family did not consume red meat at all), and shellfish were never to be eaten. We were taught to make plant-based meals that included tofu, texturized vegetable protein (TVP), and MorningStar Farms products. So, while I learned to prepare and appreciate traditional soul food from my nana, the lessons I learned from my mostly vegetarian parents became the keys to a successful transition to veganism later in life.

In 2009, I opened my own catering company specializing in soul food. I adopted my nana's Sunday soul food tradition of inviting all my friends and family over for Sunday dinners, which were usually heavy on meat and dairy at that time. Planning and cooking these weekly Sunday meals was the highlight of my week.

Shortly before my thirty-sixth birthday, I was given a diagnosis of hypertension and borderline type 2 diabetes, which the doctor said came from hereditary genes, as my mother, aunts, and grandmother all had been diagnosed with these diseases in the past. Refusing to believe that I should take pills for the rest of my life, I began to research how to heal myself, eventually arriving at the profound conclusion that meat and dairy were primary sources of my diagnosed ailments.

As a mother, chef, and entrepreneur, this pivotal moment forced me to question everything. I knew I wanted to remove animal products from my diet, but what would I eat? The answer is found in this cookbook, a culmination of years of experience—recipes I've created, influenced by my dad, my mom, and my nana's magical, soulful hands. Together, we have transformed our treasured, traditional soul food into healthier and amazingly delicious vegan soul food!

Chapter One
What Is Soul Food?

Black-Eyed Pea Salad, *page 80*

*S*oul food was created by the West African people who were stolen and brought as enslaved people to America. The term "soul food" was not actually created until the 1960s during the civil rights movement. It was born of a strong sense of pride within the black community. Even though the term was coined only somewhat recently, the cuisine has been around for a long time.

Soul food flavors and dishes are versatile, partly because of the movement of enslaved people who often were moved around throughout the South, from the Carolinas to Alabama to Tennessee. Creole and Gullah cuisines are examples of soul food variations that developed with the movement of enslaved people who used whatever native ingredients were readily available to create flavorful, soulful food to feed themselves and their families. The resiliency of enslaved people was shown by their ability to use unwanted scraps such as pig intestines, ears, and feet to create flavorful, hearty meals. As enslaved people were moved from place to place, soul food cuisine expanded. Enslaved people merged their own food knowledge with French and European influences, resulting in many now-classic dishes such as gumbo, jambalaya, and chowder.

Over the years, soul food and other southern styles of cooking were deemed unhealthy. Soul food was known as a poor man's diet. The popularity of heavily fried, highly processed, and sugar-loaded foods, along with a lack of access to fresh vegetables and fruits, has contributed to a rise in illnesses like heart disease, hypertension, and diabetes within the African American community. According to the Centers for Disease Control and Prevention (CDC), African Americans ages 18 to 49 are twice as likely to die from heart disease as whites, and African Americans ages 35 to 64 are 50 percent more likely to have high blood pressure. The recipes I've created in this book prove that soul food doesn't have to be loaded with meat and dairy or be deep-fried or sugar-coated to be comforting and delicious. After trying these recipes, you'll feel happier, more energized, and on the road to a healthier you.

I use two definitions of soul food to guide my work and my own eating. The first is the acronym SOUL: Seasonal, Organic, Unprocessed, Local. Eating foods that are seasonally grown, organic when possible, unprocessed or whole, and grown locally will go a long way toward helping you become the healthiest version of yourself. The standard American diet (SAD) tends to be high in processed convenience foods and is often high in unhealthy fats, sugars, and chemical additives. Eating the SAD way has proven to be detrimental to our health, our planet, and the lives of millions of innocent animals, so I say, let's eat the SOUL way.

My second definition of soul food is more of an energy or feeling that should be a central part of making soul food. Soul food has to be made with the love and energy of the soul poured into each dish. Soul food can't be created by just anyone. You must put love, passion, and joy into every step to make the food truly soulful. Soul food is pure love on a plate!

Veganizing Soul Food

Soul food gets a bad rap because it's typically filled with unhealthy ingredients like butter, sugar, and meat and can use unhealthy preparations like deep-frying. In this cookbook, you'll discover that most of the recipes consist of whole-food, plant-based ingredients that are fairly easy to find. Most vegans I know didn't become vegan because they woke up one day and decided they didn't like the taste of meat or dairy. Most chose this lifestyle for health reasons and because of the senseless murder of millions of animals on a daily basis. All that death just so we can eat! Creating vegan soul food was important for me to prove to myself that I could still have all my favorite comfort foods without harming any animals. By creating compassionate food, we not only save lives, but we also greatly decrease our carbon footprint and help save the planet as well.

Veganizing soul food has been such a fun and tasty process. Being able to research and play around with so many exciting and new (to me) plant-based ingredients has opened a new door of creativity in the kitchen. The vegan lifestyle has recently gained popularity, as evidenced by the huge rise in vegan products that are readily available at most supermarkets. For some people, buying mock meats and other prepared vegan foods can help with the transition to a vegan lifestyle. However, many of these foods are highly processed and not necessarily healthy. If you're transitioning into veganism or just looking to eat healthier, I recommend limiting mock meats and other prepared foods. Instead, I encourage you to visit your local farmer's market and experiment with fresh vegetables and fruits to incorporate into your new lifestyle.

The dishes and recipes compiled in this cookbook were specifically designed to pay homage to classic soul food staples while using healthier ingredients and cooking techniques and without compromising the delicious flavors of traditional soul food. One of my goals in writing this book was to show the world how healthy, delicious, and amazing vegan soul food can be. I can't guarantee that every recipe in this book is 100 percent healthy, but I can guarantee that by replacing meat and dairy with plant-based ingredients, my version is healthier than the original. For example, my Buffalo Popcorn Chickenless Bites recipe on page 94 is made with tofu, which is high in protein and is a great replacement for chicken lovers.

Veganism and Health

People eat meat and think they will become strong as an ox, forgetting that the ox eats grass. —Giuseppe Caruso

"Why go vegan?" is a question I get asked almost daily. My answer is that going vegan not only lowers your risk of developing chronic illness and disease, it also helps reduce our carbon footprint and save the lives of animals. I initially chose to go vegan to see whether it would help cure my hypertension and borderline type 2 diabetes. Much to my surprise, within my first 30 days of going vegan, my blood sugar levels and blood pressure levels normalized, and I no longer had to take prescription medication daily. I was amazed! Many studies have shown that heavy consumption of meat and dairy products is directly linked to chronic illnesses including cancer, hypertension, heart disease, type 2 diabetes, and more. A recent study initiated by the American Heart Association concluded that following a vegan diet for five weeks may decrease risk factors for heart disease, the leading killer of all Americans.

In African American communities today, it is common to have one or more family members or close friends who have been diagnosed with type 2 diabetes, cancer, or hypertension. Why are these diseases so common in our communities over others? The common link seems to be diet. Food is a big part of African American culture and community, but unfortunately, many of us have learned unhealthy ways of cooking that have been passed down from generation to generation. According to *U.S. News & World Report*, a recent study in *JAMA* concluded that the high-fat, high-sugar, high-sodium traditional southern diet leads to hypertension and heart disease and may be linked to high incidences of these illnesses in the African American community. I think it's time we try a new and better lifestyle that will contribute to extending our lives and strengthening our communities by giving our bodies the pure and natural foods they desire.

Vegan diets can also help protect against certain cancers and stabilize blood sugars, reducing the risk of developing diabetes. I personally was greatly influenced by the documentary *What the Health*. This movie really helped me understand the damage that consuming animal products inflicts on our bodies.

Since we are talking about veganism and health, I think it's important to include the health of our planet. Animal agriculture is the single largest contributor of harmful emissions and is breaking down the ozone layers in the atmosphere. In order to raise animals for mass consumption, we have cut down massive sections of the rain forest, and this has greatly contributed to wildlife extinction. Our false belief that we need to feed ourselves using animals is literally killing not only us but millions of innocent beings and the planet we all share.

If you want to live longer and be healthier, start by eating more plant-based foods. We can make a difference in our health and our world, starting with our food choices. Let's eat to live!

Healthy Vegan Guidelines

These practical tips will help you maintain a healthy vegan lifestyle.

Read Labels. Avoiding animal products is crucial when transitioning. You'll be surprised how many of your favorite foods have some form of animal product in them. Some animal by-products have names that may not be familiar at first, like whey, whey powder, casein, lactose, and gelatin. I always read the ingredients, and sometimes the bottom of the ingredient list will say whether there are milk or dairy products included. All necessary protein and nutrients needed for the body can be found in plant forms. Animals get their protein from plants, so just bypass the middleman and get all your vitamins, nutrients, and protein directly from the source.

Eat the Rainbow. Not only will eating vegetables of all different colors help make your dishes vibrant and beautiful, but each color fruit or vegetable has phytonutrients that basically are the nutrients of that fruit or vegetable. Red fruits and vegetables like tomatoes, red peppers, and strawberries have vitamins A and C, antioxidants, and manganese. Green vegetables and fruits like broccoli, cabbage, cucumbers, and kale contain vitamins B and K, folate, and potassium. Orange vegetables and fruits like carrots, oranges, sweet potatoes, and cantaloupe contain vitamins C, A, and B_6, as well as antioxidants. Purple vegetables and fruits like eggplant, red onions, purple potatoes, plums, and blueberries contain B vitamins and antioxidants. White produce such as cauliflower, garlic, mushrooms, and potatoes contains vitamins K and C. If you eat a variety of colors on your plate each week, you are more likely to get the vitamins and nutrients your body needs.

Follow the 80/20 Rule. You'll hear this frequently in health-conscious communities. I love this rule primarily because it allows you to eat healthy 80 percent of the time and indulge in small amounts of fried or processed foods and desserts the other 20 percent of the time. This gives you a great balance, and you really don't feel like you're missing anything.

Turn Up the Flavor. One of the most important things in going vegan is to have a happy palate. Adding fresh herbs and using a creative variety of seasoning blends will go a long way toward making your mouth smile. Embrace the vegan whole-food, plant-based lifestyle by getting creative with vegetables and fruits. You'll consume everything your body needs through plants, legumes, nuts, fruits, and grains.

How to Cook from This Book

On this cooking journey we are about to embark on, you can expect to learn easy and creative techniques to transform traditional soul food favorites into healthier versions. We'll discuss some history and origins of southern staples and explore how and what is needed to veganize these dishes. Then we will explore the health benefits and nutritional value of staple vegan ingredients and how they are used. Next is the fun part. We get to play with food! I have shared 101 plant-based vegan soul food recipes in this book for you to experiment with and enjoy.

All recipes include labels like gluten-free, oil-free, nut-free, or soy-free. Dishes that can be prepared in 30 minutes or less are labeled, too. In the following pages, you will find some key general information to set you up for success on this vegan soul food journey. Happy cooking!

Improvise

The wonderful thing about creating in the kitchen is the ability to improvise. This is one reason cooking tops baking for me. Baking has to be precise, but with cooking you can add additional ingredients if you feel like your recipe is missing something. I'd highly suggest that you try all the recipes as instructed once; then when you have a good idea of the taste and flavor profile you're looking for, feel free to play around with different ingredients to create your own take. For example, the Caribbean Coconut Greens recipe on page 62 can be made with less coconut cream if you're not a big fan of coconut flavor, or you can increase the amount of liquid smoke to give it a stronger smoky taste. It really just depends on what your palate likes and how creative you'd like to get. With most recipes, some ingredients can be switched out depending on what ingredients you might already have on hand. Soul food is the perfect food to get creative with. Infuse it with love and make it your own.

Southern Staples

There are certain staple ingredients that go along with any regional cuisine. In this section, I list and describe some of the key staples that will be used in the recipes that follow.

Vegetables

Corn or maize dates back at least 6,000 years and evolved from teosinte, which is a wild grass. Corn was developed by ancient Mexicans, adopted by Native Americans, and easily accessible to enslaved people because it was cheap and easy to grow. Corn is rich in vitamin B_1 and vitamin C and has a good amount of fiber. Since corn production in the United States has greatly increased over the past century, it is now mass-produced, and I recommend purchasing organic, non-GMO (genetically modified organism) corn if possible.

Collards are the oldest members of the cabbage family and were grown by the ancient Greeks. Collards are a good source of protein and fiber and also contain folic acid, vitamin A, vitamin C, calcium, potassium, iron, and zinc. Collards were known as a poor man's food during slavery and remain inexpensive. They are usually cooked with other greens like mustard, turnip, dandelion, or kale. Collards have large leaves, are slightly bitter, and can be on the tougher side.

Kale is considered a superfood because of its amazing nutrient density. It's high in fiber, protein, and vitamins A, C, and K and contains folate, which is great for brain development. Kale is not as tough as collard greens and is a great addition to soups, stews, salads, burgers, and smoothies.

Dandelion greens are high in vitamins A, C, and K. This green helps the absorption of iron. It also contains essential and trace minerals. This bitter green should be used in smaller amounts in salads so the strong taste does not overpower the dish.

Sweet potato is a root vegetable and was a staple ingredient for African enslaved people. Sweet potatoes are sweet, starchy, and rich in vitamins, antioxidants, fiber, and minerals. Sweet potatoes can be used in many dishes, from pies to soups to casseroles.

Cabbage contains potassium, vitamin B_1, fiber, folate, manganese, and vitamin B_6. Fried cabbage will always be a favorite dish of mine. Find my recipe on page 74.

Green beans, also known as pole beans, are high in folate, thiamin, riboflavin, iron, magnesium, and potassium. These delicious beans are thought to have originated in Central America and are now very popular in southern-style cooking.

Fruits

Watermelon grows well in the southern states and became known as a poor man's food because enslaved people were able to grow, eat, and sell it after emancipation. Watermelon is sweet, juicy, and hydrating, along with being high in vitamins C and A, antioxidants, and potassium. When in season, watermelon is my favorite fruit. Watermelon barbecue sauce, fresh watermelon juice, and adding watermelon to salads are just a few ways to use this delicious fruit.

Peaches are soft, juicy, and fragrant. They grow abundantly in all of the southern states, and, of course, Georgia is known for its amazing sweet peaches. If you love peaches, wait until you try my Peaches and Cream French Toast on page 21.

Blackberries grow abundantly across the United States. They are high in fiber, antioxidants, and vitamin K and can easily be made into syrup, cobblers, jams, or preserves.

Plums were brought to America around the seventeenth century. They are high in fiber and natural sugar that doesn't spike blood sugar. Plums are a tasty addition to salads, are great as a snack, and can be made into sweet and savory sauces.

Beans and Legumes

Lima beans or butter beans have a sweet, smooth, and buttery flavor that has made them very popular in southern-style cooking. These beans pair well with corn and potatoes and are a great addition to soups and stews.

Black-eyed peas or cowpeas are one of the most well-known ingredients in soul food cuisine. These beans originated in West Africa and arrived in America sometime in the 1700s. They are traditionally cooked in an African American home during the holidays and especially at New Year's, as they are a symbol of good luck and prosperity. They are high in protein, iron, and fiber.

Kidney beans are another staple in soul food cuisine. They show up in such common dishes as rice and beans or chili. These red beans are high in vitamins and minerals and are a great source of protein.

Lentils are one of my favorites and are the most versatile pulses for vegan cooking. Lentils are small in size but hearty in texture and flavor, making them a terrific meat replacement. This tiny bean is a nutrient powerhouse, leading the way in protein among legumes and also containing potassium, folate, iron, and fiber. Try my Peach-Habanero Barbecue Lentil Mini Loaves on page 91.

Peanuts, or groundnuts, were brought to America by enslaved people from West Africa in the 1700s. Even though "nut" is in the name, peanuts are actually legumes. Peanuts are high in fiber, protein, healthy fats, magnesium, calcium, and iron. Boiled peanuts are a southern favorite passed down from West African enslaved people.

Spices

Dried thyme is a savory pungent herb that is used a lot in Caribbean cooking. You'll see this wonderful spice in many recipes in this book. Thyme has a unique earthy flavor that blends wonderfully in soul food.

White pepper has a mild but distinct flavor. Black and white pepper are used for different flavoring purposes in soul cooking. White pepper should be used in more lightly seasoned recipes like my Plum-Tahini Dressing on page 127.

Cayenne or red pepper is spicy and is used to add a kick to many soul food, Caribbean, and Creole dishes.

Kelp powder comes from a sea vegetable that is high in potassium, magnesium, calcium, iron, and iodine. Kelp, or nori, has a sea taste and is ideal to use in recipes like my Cajun Crabless Jackfruit Balls on page 63 or my Fishless Banana-Blossom Fish on page 98.

Apple cider vinegar is derived from fermented apple juice. Fermented foods have good gut bacteria in them that aid in digestion. Look for brands that are organic and that have the cloudy "mother" in them. I use this ingredient in several baking recipes as well as in dressings, marinades, and sauces. Apple cider vinegar improves heart health, assists in stabilizing blood sugar, aids in weight loss, kills harmful gut bacteria, and lowers cholesterol.

Nutritional yeast or "nooch" is inactive yeast that can be grown on blackstrap molasses or sugar beets. It has a light, buttery, cheesy flavor and is high in protein, fiber, minerals, and vitamins. Nooch is commonly used in vegan cooking to replace the flavor of cheese. It's great on popcorn, in macaroni and cheese, in sauces, or as a topping on salads.

Bay leaves have a soft, floral, somewhat earthy tone. Bay leaves are commonly used in soups, stews, rice dishes, and cooked grains.

Onion powder has a more concentrated taste compared to onions. Fresh onions and onion powder are commonly used to maximize flavor profiles in southern vegan cooking.

Liquid smoke is one of my favorite ingredients to use in soulful cooking. It adds that full, round flavor of smokiness that is truly needed in vegan soul food. I use this spice in many dishes, like my Smoky Tempeh Bacon on page 17, and my Three-Bean Chili on page 52.

Smoked paprika can have a variety of heat levels, from mild to spicy. I usually look for a milder version, because the smoky flavor stands out more in dishes. The smoky undertones in this spice are a wonderful complement in vegan soul food cooking.

Granulated garlic is a coarse grade of dried garlic that I prefer to use in most recipes, as I have found that the flavor profile is stronger than garlic powder. Garlic is a good source of iron, copper, manganese, and phosphorus.

Sweeteners

Cane sugar has long been associated with slavery, beginning in the Caribbean. Settlers first brought cane sugar to America, specifically Louisiana, around the 1700s. White sugar is cane sugar that has been refined using animal bone char to remove any impurities. This is not vegan and should be avoided. Organic cane sugar is what is usually found in my pantry.

Maple syrup is a wonderful, tasty sweetener derived from the sap of maple trees that traditionally grow in the northern states. It is a great ingredient for southern cuisine and baking and can be used in place of corn syrups, which are highly processed and mass-produced.

Brown sugar is simply cane sugar that has kept some of the natural molasses during refinement. Brown sugar is delicious in baking, sauces, and dressings.

Coconut sugar is a low-glycemic sugar made from the sap of the coconut palm. This sugar can be used as a 1:1 replacement for brown sugar in many baking recipes.

Molasses has the lowest sugar content of cane sugars. It is a thick, dark syrup that is made by boiling down cane sugar or sugar beets. This syrup is high in iron, calcium, and magnesium and is great in baking or making sauces.

Agave nectar is harvested from the core of the agave plant and usually comes from Mexico. This sweetener is a great replacement for honey and is good for diabetics because it does not spike blood sugar as much as cane sugar does.

Pantry

- **Vegetable stock cubes** are used to add flavor and seasoning to many dishes in this cookbook. These cubes can be fairly high in sodium, so beware if adding additional salt.

- **Ground flax meal** is used as a binder in many recipes in this cookbook. Mixing flax meal with water creates a thick liquid called a "flax egg," which is used in vegan baking.

- **Coconut cream** is a thicker version of coconut milk. I use this in soups, stews, and baking.

- **Almond milk** is my favorite nut milk option. I believe it to taste most like cow's milk out of all the nut milks.

- **Tamari** is a gluten-free soy sauce that can be used in place of salt in many sauces.

- **Earth Balance** is my favorite vegan butter. I've tried most of the ones out there, and this one has just the right

amount of water content and makes baking a breeze.

- **Grapeseed oil** can be used in dressings, frying, sautéing, and baking. This is a high-heat oil and is recommended for alkaline cooking.

- **Sunflower oil** is a light oil that I like to use for dressings, sauces, frying, and baking.

- **Unbleached all-purpose flour** should be stored in a sealed container. Bob's Red Mill Gluten-Free 1-to-1 Baking Flour can be used as a replacement flour if you want to make some of the recipes in this book gluten-free.

- **Baking soda** is a leavener, which means it helps dough rise and makes baked goods fluffy.

- **Baking powder** is also a leavener but has a much lighter taste.

- **Cornmeal** is finely ground corn that is used in batters, corn bread, and my favorite, hush puppies.

- **Firm or extra-firm tofu** is made from soybeans and is used commonly in vegan cooking. I use it as a scrambled-egg replacement or for mock "chicken" bits. It needs to be refrigerated.

- **Panko bread crumbs** are Japanese bread crumbs that give a perfectly crunchy coating to cauliflower wings, avocado fries, and more.

- **Tempeh** is fermented tofu that is used mainly as a bacon replacement in this cookbook, but it can be used in a variety of vegan recipes.

- **Textured vegetable protein** or TVP is freeze-dried tofu granules. It is great in vegan burgers, sausage, pot pies, and more to add protein and meaty texture.

- **Applesauce** is used in this cookbook as a replacement for eggs. I use ⅓ cup applesauce per egg for a super-moist dessert.

- **Just Mayo and Best Foods Vegan Mayo** are my favorites in the vegan mayo department. They are the closest to regular mayonnaise in flavor and texture and can be used just as you would nonvegan brands.

- **Grits** are made with finely ground white corn and are a staple in southern cuisine.

- **Pecans** are commonly used in soul food baking. They have a buttery taste and are mainly cultivated in Georgia, Texas, and Mexico.

- **Canned diced tomatoes** are a quick and easy way to add flavor and depth to many recipes, especially soups and stews.

- **Tomato paste** is a thick paste made by slow-cooking tomatoes with the seeds and skin strained out. This paste is great to thicken, flavor, and enhance dishes.

- **Potatoes** play a big role in soul food— for example, in recipes like Cajun Potato Salad on page 36, and Garlic-Smashed Potatoes on page 71

- **Brown basmati rice** is something I prefer over regular brown rice because it is more fragrant, takes less time to cook, and is hard to overcook.

- **Vital wheat gluten** is a protein that is extracted from wheat. It is over 80 percent protein and is used to make many commercial mock meats.

So now that we have covered the what, why, and how of veganism and soul food, it's time to let the fun begin. Next, you'll find all the vegan soul food recipes you'll need to assist you on this journey to a healthier, more compassionate, more soulful you!

Peaches and Cream French Toast, *page 21*

Chapter Two

Breakfast

Farmhouse Scramble

GLUTEN-FREE, NUT-FREE, 30 MINUTES OR LESS

SERVES 4 • PREP TIME: 10 MINUTES • COOK TIME: 15 MINUTES

FOR THE SEASONING BLEND

1 teaspoon turmeric

**½ teaspoon
smoked paprika**

**1 teaspoon
granulated garlic**

½ teaspoon onion powder

**¼ teaspoon freshly ground
black pepper**

1 teaspoon cumin

½ teaspoon curry powder

¼ teaspoon chili powder

FOR THE SCRAMBLE

1 tablespoon tamari

**1 (16-ounce) package firm
tofu, drained**

1 tablespoon grapeseed oil

⅓ cup red onions, diced

**⅓ cup colored bell
peppers, diced**

**6 shiitake mushrooms,
thinly sliced**

1 garlic clove, minced

**⅓ cup roughly
chopped kale**

**⅓ cup roughly chopped
Swiss chard**

This hearty, protein-packed scramble is a wonderful replacement for scrambled eggs and reminds me of the weekend breakfasts we made growing up. Eggs are inexpensive, but tofu is even cheaper and makes a delicious meal that will keep you full for hours.

1. Mix together the turmeric, paprika, granulated garlic, onion powder, black pepper, cumin, curry powder, and chili powder. Set the seasoning mix aside.

2. In a medium bowl, mash the drained tofu with a masher or by hand to make crumbles.

3. After the tofu is crumbled, add the seasoning mixture. Mix well and set aside.

4. In a medium sauté pan over medium-high heat, heat the oil; then add the onions, bell peppers, and mushrooms and stir.

5. Allow the vegetables to cook for 3 to 4 minutes, until the onions are slightly translucent; then add the garlic and tamari, and stir. Allow to cook for 1 minute.

6. Add the seasoned tofu. Cook, stirring often, for a few minutes. Then add the kale and Swiss chard and stir.

7. Cook for 4 to 5 minutes, or until the kale has softened. Remove from the heat and serve.

....

Tip: This recipe will work with almost any vegetables you have on hand and is great topped with diced tomato and avocado. Use leftovers to make breakfast burritos.

Smoky Tempeh Bacon

GLUTEN-FREE, NUT-FREE, OIL-FREE, 30 MINUTES OR LESS

SERVES 4 TO 6 • PREP TIME: 12 MINUTES • COOK TIME: 12 MINUTES

1 (8-ounce) package tempeh
¼ cup tamari
¼ cup maple syrup
1½ tablespoons liquid smoke

Believe me, you won't miss regular bacon after tasting this vegan version. I usually have to make a double batch of these babies, because they are gone before I can even add them to a breakfast sandwich. You can swap out the tempeh if you're trying to stay away from soy and use unsweetened coconut flakes, eggplant slices, or king oyster mushrooms instead. This bacon is a great addition to almost any recipe and is especially great as a side dish with waffles or corn cakes.

1. Preheat the oven to 400°F.

2. Slice the tempeh into ½-inch-thick strips and place them in an 8-by-10-inch baking pan.

3. In a medium bowl, whisk together the tamari, maple syrup, and liquid smoke.

4. Pour the marinade over the tempeh, and let sit for 10 minutes, turning each piece after 5 minutes so that both sides are coated.

5. Bake for 6 minutes, then turn each piece of tempeh over and bake for another 6 minutes.

6. Remove from the oven and let cool for 2 to 3 minutes before serving.

....

Tip: Crumble cooked tempeh bacon to use as a salad topping or in gravy for Biscuits and Gravy (page 20).

Maple-Sage Breakfast Sausage

NUT-FREE, OIL-FREE, 30 MINUTES OR LESS

MAKES 8 LARGE PATTIES • PREP TIME: 15 MINUTES • COOK TIME: 15 MINUTES, PLUS TIME TO COOL

Nonstick cooking spray

¾ cup textured vegetable protein (TVP)

¾ cup boiling hot water

3 tablespoons flax meal

⅓ cup water

¼ cup nutritional yeast

4 tablespoons maple syrup

1 teaspoon dried thyme

2 to 3 teaspoons ground sage

1 tablespoon garlic powder

1 teaspoon onion powder

Pinch cayenne pepper

2 tablespoons tamari

¼ cup flour, plus more as needed

You won't believe how simple and tasty these breakfast sausages are! They take me on a trip down memory lane. When I was a child, my father would make some amazing dishes with textured vegetable protein (TVP), and I loved to watch him create magic in the kitchen with these little granules. TVP also can be used to replace ground beef in tacos, chili, or pasta dishes. I used TVP even when I wasn't vegan, and people never knew they were eating a meatless dish. You can find TVP in the health food section in most grocery stores. Look for Bob's Red Mill products, as they are usually grouped together. If you're unable to locate it at your grocery store, you can order it online.

1. Preheat the oven to 400°F. Line a baking pan with parchment paper or coat with cooking spray.

2. In a medium bowl, cover the TVP with the hot water and stir. Cover and set aside for 5 minutes.

3. In a small bowl, mix the flax meal and ⅓ cup water with a fork or whisk to create a "flax egg." Let the mixture sit for 5 to 7 minutes to thicken.

4. Uncover the TVP and stir with a large spoon, then add the nutritional yeast, maple syrup, thyme, sage, garlic powder, onion powder, cayenne pepper, tamari, and flour, along with the flax egg mixture.

5. Stir the mixture for 1 to 2 minutes, then test your mixture by taking about 1 tablespoon and forming it into a ball in your hands. The mixture should not be too loose. If it is, add a little more flour and mix again.

6. Remove the lid from a large mason jar. Hold the lid upside down in the palm of your hand and pack it tightly with the TVP mixture, making sure it is not overflowing and has a smooth surface.

7. Turn the packed lid over onto the prepared baking pan and lightly push through the lid hole to release the patty.

8. Repeat this process to make a total of 8 patties, then place the baking pan into the oven and bake for 6 to 7 minutes. Turn the patties over and bake for another 6 to 7 minutes.

9. The patties are ready when they are browned and slightly crispy. Remove from the oven, and let cool for 2 to 3 minutes before serving.

Tip: For a crispier patty, pan-fry for 2 to 3 minutes on each side instead of baking. For more flavor and texture, try adding diced apples to the mixture. To make smaller patties, use a lid from a smaller mason jar.

Tip: These patties are terrific in a sausage biscuit sandwich. Make my Buttermilk Biscuits (page 132); add lettuce, sliced tomato, sliced onion, and your favorite vegan cheese; and then top with my Cajun Chipotle Aioli (page 126) to make the ultimate breakfast sandwich.

Biscuits and Gravy

NUT-FREE

MAKES 8 BISCUITS · PREP TIME: 15 MINUTES · COOK TIME: 20 MINUTES

4½ tablespoons
   sunflower oil
½ teaspoon salt
½ teaspoon freshly ground
   black pepper
1½ teaspoons dried thyme
2 teaspoons
   granulated garlic
1 teaspoon onion powder
4½ tablespoons
   unbleached
   all-purpose flour
3 cups water or
   plant-based milk
1 batch Buttermilk Biscuits
   (page 132)
2 tablespoons chopped
   flat-leaf parsley

This recipe is a true southern classic. Fresh biscuits appeared regularly in my nana's house, and we loved it when she would serve them with sausage gravy. When veganizing this recipe, I knew I needed to make sure that the buttery, crispy outside and warm, fluffy inside were carried over from Nana's recipe. Enjoy!

1. In a medium sauté pan, heat the oil over medium-high heat; then add the salt, black pepper, thyme, granulated garlic, and onion powder and stir to combine. Turn the heat down to low and sauté for 3 to 5 minutes.

2. Stir in the flour until well combined and allow to lightly brown; then add the water and stir.

3. Cook for 5 to 8 minutes, to desired thickness.

4. Plate the biscuits, pour the gravy over the top, and garnish with the parsley to serve.

Tip: To add more texture to the gravy, add crumbled Maple-Sage Breakfast Sausage (page 18) or Smoky Tempeh Bacon (page 17). If the gravy is too thin, stir in a couple tablespoons of flour and allow to thicken.

Peaches and Cream French Toast

NUT-FREE, 30 MINUTES OR LESS

SERVES 4 • PREP TIME: 10 MINUTES • COOK TIME: 15 MINUTES

FOR THE WHIPPED CREAM

1 (15-ounce) can coconut whipping cream, kept in refrigerator overnight

2 tablespoons maple syrup

FOR THE SAUCE

2 or 3 fresh peaches, washed and sliced, or 8 ounces frozen peaches, thawed

⅓ teaspoon cinnamon

½ teaspoon vanilla

1 tablespoon brown sugar

½ tablespoon cane sugar

1 tablespoon Earth Balance vegan butter

FOR THE FRENCH TOAST

¼ cup chickpea flour

½ teaspoon ground cinnamon

½ teaspoon vanilla extract

2 tablespoons brown sugar

¾ cup plant-based milk

1 tablespoon Earth Balance vegan butter

4 to 6 slices whole-grain bread

When you start your morning off with a delicious, filling breakfast, you feel like you can conquer the world. I created this recipe some years ago when my children were still small. Saturday mornings in my house included a smorgasbord of breakfast dishes for my boys. This dish was always the first to disappear. When peaches are in season, try white peaches for an even sweeter dish.

To make the whipped cream

1. Remove the can of coconut cream from the refrigerator. Chilling the cream thickens the liquid, which helps the whipping process.

2. Place the cream in a deep mixing bowl and add the maple syrup.

3. Using a handheld mixer, whip on maximum speed for 3 to 4 minutes, until the cream is thick and forms peaks.

4. Put the bowl back into the refrigerator until the other recipe components are done.

To make the sauce

1. In a medium mixing bowl, stir together the peaches, cinnamon, vanilla, brown sugar, and cane sugar and set aside.

Continued

Peaches and Cream French Toast *Continued*

2. Melt the butter in a medium saucepan over medium heat; then add the peach mixture and stir. Cover and allow to cook for 6 to 8 minutes or until the peaches are tender and a caramel sauce has developed and thickened.

3. Turn off the heat and keep the sauce covered.

To make the French toast

1. In a medium mixing bowl, whisk together the chickpea flour, cinnamon, vanilla, brown sugar, and ¾ cup of milk.

2. Heat a skillet over medium heat, then add the butter and allow it to melt. While the butter is melting, dip the bread slices into the chickpea mixture. Turn to coat both sides, shake off any excess batter, and place the bread in the hot skillet.

3. Cook until golden brown; then flip to cook the other side.

4. Remove the toast from the skillet and transfer to a plate. Top with the peach mixture and a dollop of whipped cream. Repeat with all of the remaining bread slices. Serve immediately.

Smoky Grits with Cajun "Butter" and Roasted Vegetables

GLUTEN-FREE, NUT-FREE, 30 MINUTES OR LESS

SERVES 4 TO 6 • PREP TIME: 10 MINUTES • COOK TIME: 15 MINUTES

1 cup diced zucchini

1 cup diced yellow squash

8 stems asparagus, cut into 6-inch pieces

½ cup button mushrooms, sliced thick

½ red onion, diced

½ cup diced bell peppers

2 tablespoons grapeseed or sunflower oil

3 pinches sea salt, divided

3 cups water

3 cups plant-based milk

1½ cups quick grits

½ teaspoon liquid smoke

3 tablespoons Earth Balance vegan butter

1½ teaspoons Creole Cajun Seasoning (page 123)

Southern cuisine is known for grits. Some like them sweet, while others, like me, like them savory. Grits are basically a less-starchy corn dried and ground to make tiny granules. When I was growing up, grits and Cream of Wheat were the two main hot cereals I could almost always find in the cabinet. My recipe is a savory flavor–packed bowl of goodness!

1. Preheat the oven to 425°F. Line a baking pan with parchment paper.

2. In a medium mixing bowl, stir together the zucchini, yellow squash, asparagus, mushrooms, onion, bell peppers, oil, and 1 pinch of salt.

3. Spread the veggies on the lined baking pan and roast for 10 to 12 minutes.

4. In a medium saucepan, bring the water and milk to a boil. Add the remaining 2 pinches of salt; then slowly add the grits, stirring continuously. Cover and reduce the heat to low. Stir occasionally for 5 to 6 minutes. The grits will be done when they become thick and creamy.

5. Once the grits are soft, turn off the heat, add the liquid smoke, stir, and cover.

6. Remove the veggies from the oven and allow to cool.

Continued

7. In a small saucepan over low heat, melt the butter, add the Cajun seasoning, and stir.

8. To serve, spoon the grits into a bowl and top with the roasted veggies and Cajun butter.

....

Tip: Swap out the vegetables for fruit and brown sugar to make a sweeter version of this breakfast. Grits can be stored in the refrigerator for 2 to 3 days. Reheat by adding a little milk or water and whisking the grits in a saucepan over low heat.

Sweet Potato Quinoa Pancakes

GLUTEN-FREE, NUT-FREE, SOY-FREE, 30 MINUTES OR LESS

SERVES 4 • PREP TIME: 8 MINUTES • COOK TIME: 15 MINUTES

1 cup gluten-free flour

⅓ cup sweet potato purée

1 tablespoon grapeseed or
   sunflower oil

¾ tablespoon
   baking powder

½ teaspoon cinnamon

1 tablespoon flax meal

½ teaspoon vanilla extract

½ cup cooked quinoa

1½ teaspoons agave nectar

Pinch sea salt

Nonstick cooking spray

The addition of sweet potato makes these pancakes extra moist, while adding quinoa gives you a protein and fiber boost to start your day. This recipe is a great way to use leftover sweet potatoes and quinoa, which also helps cut down on cooking time. Add a side of Smoky Tempeh Bacon (page 17) or Maple-Sage Breakfast Sausage (page 18) for a real southern breakfast experience.

1. Preheat the oven to the lowest setting, about 140°F.

2. In a medium mixing bowl, whisk together all the ingredients except the cooking spray until well combined. Set aside for 5 minutes.

3. Heat a griddle or nonstick pan and use the cooking spray to evenly coat the surface.

4. Once the griddle is nice and hot, spoon about ⅓ cup of the pancake mixture onto it to form each pancake. Usually 3 pancakes can cook at a time.

5. When the pancakes begin to form air bubbles, usually after about 4 minutes, check that the bottoms are golden brown; then flip and allow to cook for another 3 to 4 minutes.

6. Transfer the pancakes to the oven to keep warm while you finish cooking the remaining pancakes.

Tip: Top these pancakes with a dollop of vegan butter, fresh berries, and maple syrup. They will keep in the refrigerator in a sealed container for 2 to 3 days.

Peanut Butter Green Smoothie Bowl

GLUTEN-FREE, OIL-FREE, SOY-FREE, 30 MINUTES OR LESS

SERVES 4 • PREP TIME: 10 MINUTES

2 cups coconut milk

2 ripe bananas

8 pitted dates

1 ripe avocado

2 handfuls spinach or
   baby kale

4 tablespoons
   peanut butter

2 tablespoons hemp hearts

1½ to 2 cups ice

I have smoothies most days for breakfast. They are not only satisfying but also a great way to have something quick, healthy, and protein-packed that will fuel you for hours. A smoothie bowl is just a thicker smoothie poured into a bowl and topped with a variety of sliced fruit, granola, nuts, and seeds.

1. Place all the ingredients in a high-powered blender and blend on medium-high for 2 to 3 minutes or until well combined.

2. Pour the smoothie into a medium serving bowl and top with your choice of toppings.

Tip: For a sweeter smoothie, add 1 tablespoon of agave nectar. If you are in the mood for some chocolate, add 2 to 3 tablespoons of 100 percent cacao powder. Try topping with sliced bananas, chia seeds, mixed berries, or shredded coconut.

Loaded Sweet Potato Hash

GLUTEN-FREE, NUT-FREE, 30 MINUTES OR LESS

SERVES 4 TO 6 • PREP TIME: 15 MINUTES • COOK TIME: 15 MINUTES

1 medium sweet potato,
    peeled and shredded

2 medium red potatoes,
    shredded

⅓ cup diced red or yellow
    bell pepper

1 medium red onion, diced

3 garlic cloves, minced

1 teaspoon sea salt

½ teaspoon
    smoked paprika

1 teaspoon onion powder

1 teaspoon dried rosemary

1 teaspoon dried thyme

1 teaspoon dried sage

1 teaspoon freshly ground
    black pepper

Pinch cayenne pepper
    (optional)

6 tablespoons grapeseed
    or sunflower oil, divided

½ cup stemmed, finely
    sliced collard greens

½ cup seasoned tofu
    (from the Farmhouse
    Scramble recipe,
    page 16)

Looking for a hearty, filling breakfast for you and the family? Here it is! This recipe provides a good balance of starches from the vegetables and protein from the tofu. When my sons were younger and busy with athletic activities, I made this dish often. This is also a great way to use up leftover tofu scramble.

1. In a medium mixing bowl, combine the shredded sweet and red potatoes, bell pepper, onion, garlic, sea salt, paprika, onion powder, rosemary, thyme, sage, black pepper, cayenne pepper (if using), and 1½ tablespoons of oil and stir to mix well.

2. Heat a griddle or cast-iron skillet over medium-high heat and add 3 tablespoons of oil. Once the oil is hot, spoon the potato mixture using a medium ice cream scoop (about 2.75 ounces) onto the griddle and flatten slightly.

3. Cook for 5 to 7 minutes or until desired crispiness. When the potato mounds are slightly crispy and turning golden brown, turn them over and move them closer together to create space on the griddle.

4. In the space on the griddle, drizzle the remaining 1½ tablespoons of oil, add the collards and tofu scramble, and sauté for 3 to 4 minutes.

5. Remove the hash mounds to a plate and top with the scramble, and collards.

Kale, Watermelon, and Apple Salad, *page 41*

Chapter Three
Salads

Collard, Apple, and Bacon Salad

GLUTEN-FREE, NUT-FREE, 30 MINUTES OR LESS

SERVES 4 TO 6 • PREP TIME: 15 MINUTES

FOR THE SALAD

4 or 5 large collard greens, stemmed and cut into thin ribbons

½ bunch dandelion greens

¼ cup red onion, thinly sliced

⅓ cup yellow bell pepper, thinly sliced

1 cup finely sliced Gala or Honeycrisp apples

⅓ cup finely shredded red cabbage or carrots

6 strips Smoky Tempeh Bacon (page 17)

FOR THE DRESSING

4 tablespoons pineapple juice

⅓ cup grapeseed or sunflower oil

1 tablespoon apple cider vinegar

1 tablespoon granulated garlic

1½ tablespoons maple syrup

This flavorful salad is one of my favorites. The collards are nicely softened by the dressing, while the apples and bacon combine for tasty bites of sweet and smoky flavor. This recipe incorporates my Smoky Tempeh Bacon (page 17). When making tempeh bacon for a weekend breakfast or brunch, I suggest doubling the batch so that you will have extra on hand for salads like this one during the week.

1. In a medium mixing bowl, combine the collard ribbons, dandelion greens, onion, bell peppers, and apples.

2. To make the dressing, in a small mixing bowl, whisk all the dressing ingredients until well combined.

3. Pour the dressing mixture over the collard mixture and lightly toss.

4. Divide the salad among 4 to 6 plates, top with a sprinkle of red cabbage and a spoonful of crumbled tempeh bacon, and serve.

Tip: Kale or Swiss chard is a great replacement for the greens, and peaches, blackberries, or blueberries can be used instead of apples. Store undressed greens and fruit in separate containers in the refrigerator for up to 2 days.

Heirloom Tomato and Avocado Stacks

NUT-FREE, SOY-FREE, 30 MINUTES OR LESS

SERVES 4 TO 6 • PREP TIME: 10 MINUTES • COOK TIME: 5 MINUTES

FOR THE DRESSING

6 tablespoons balsamic glaze

1½ tablespoons agave nectar

FOR THE STACKS

3 or 4 medium heirloom tomatoes

½ teaspoon sea salt, divided, plus a pinch

1 teaspoon white pepper, divided

4 avocados

¼ cup lime juice

½ cup grapeseed or sunflower oil

⅓ cup unbleached all-purpose flour

¼ cup red onion, thinly sliced and covered in water

If you've ever had heirloom tomatoes in season, you know how sweet and yummy they are. If you don't feel like cooking but want a refreshing, light lunch or snack, this is it. I top these stacks with fried, crispy onions.

To make the dressing

In a small mixing bowl, whisk together the balsamic glaze and agave nectar and set aside.

To make the stacks

1. Slice the tomatoes into ½-inch-thick slices; then lay them out on a 9-by-3-inch pan or tray. Sprinkle lightly with ¼ teaspoon of salt and ½ teaspoon of white pepper, making sure to sprinkle both sides of each slice.

2. Halve the avocados and then slice them into ½-inch rounds, leaving the skin on for easier slicing. Then peel the avocado slices, brush with the lime juice, and sprinkle with the remaining ¼ teaspoon of salt and the remaining ½ teaspoon of white pepper, placing them on the tray with the tomatoes.

3. On a plate, build the stacks. Start with a slice of tomato, then add a drizzle of dressing, and top with a slice of avocado. Repeat.

Continued

Heirloom Tomato and Avocado Stacks *Continued*

4. In a medium saucepan over medium heat, heat the oil.

5. In a medium mixing bowl, combine the flour and a pinch of salt. Line a plate with paper towels.

6. Remove the sliced onions from the water and shake off any excess. Toss a few slices at a time in the flour and then carefully add to the hot oil.

7. Allow the onion slices to cook for 2 to 3 minutes, or until they are slightly golden brown and crispy.

8. Use tongs or a fork to remove the onions from the oil and place on the paper towel–lined plate to dry. Top your stacks with the crispy onions. Serve immediately.

Rustic Quinoa and Peach Salad

GLUTEN-FREE, NUT-FREE, SOY-FREE, 30 MINUTES OR LESS

SERVES 4 TO 6 • PREP TIME: 10 MINUTES • COOK TIME: 20 MINUTES, IF COOKING QUINOA

FOR THE SALAD

3 cups cooked quinoa, cooled

½ cup dandelion greens, roughly chopped

½ cup stemmed, thinly sliced lacinato kale

¼ cup shredded carrots

⅓ cup halved cherry tomatoes

1 tablespoon pumpkin seeds

½ cup fresh peaches, diced

2 tablespoons thinly sliced scallions

1 tablespoon raisins

FOR THE DRESSING

¼ cup tahini

¼ cup sunflower oil

1 tablespoon granulated garlic

½ tablespoon turmeric

1 teaspoon onion powder

2 to 3 tablespoons fresh lime juice

Freshly ground black pepper, to taste

Sea salt, to taste

2 to 3 tablespoons water, or more if needed

This salad is filling, delicious, and packed with all the nutrients you need to refuel. When I lived in Georgia, I looked forward to the summer growing season because of the abundance of fruit, especially sweet peaches, watermelon, strawberries, and cherries. This salad is a great way to highlight local fruit as well as use up leftovers such as cooked quinoa and chopped vegetables.

1. In a large mixing bowl, toss all the salad ingredients together and set aside.

2. In a medium mixing bowl, whisk all the dressing ingredients together until well combined, 2 to 3 minutes.

3. Serve the salad with the dressing drizzled on top.

Avocado Slaw

GLUTEN-FREE, NUT-FREE, OIL-FREE, SOY-FREE, 30 MINUTES OR LESS

SERVES 4 TO 6 • PREP TIME: 5 MINUTES

FOR THE AVOCADO DRESSING

½ cup chopped cilantro

2 avocados

1 teaspoon sea salt, or more to taste

Freshly ground black pepper, to taste

1 or 2 garlic cloves, minced

2½ tablespoons lime juice

¾ cup water

FOR THE SLAW

1 (16-ounce) bag prepackaged coleslaw mix

Coleslaw is truly a staple in soul food. I cannot remember having any Sunday dinner without slaw and potato salad. This recipe is packed with good fats from avocados and is super easy to make. If you prefer, you can shred your own cabbage and carrots, but this recipe uses prepared slaw mix to save time. This slaw is also great topped with crispy onions and sliced jalapeño for some extra crunch and a bit of heat.

1. In a high-powered blender, blend all the dressing ingredients on medium-high for 2 to 3 minutes or until thick, creamy, and well combined.

2. In a medium bowl, combine the slaw mix and the dressing. Serve immediately.

Tip: If you are like me and prefer a fresh, crisp slaw, add the dressing right before serving to keep the cabbage from breaking down and becoming soggy. Store the slaw and dressing separately in the refrigerator for 2 to 3 days.

Tip: If there is any dressing left over, store it refrigerated in a sealed container for 3 days. This dressing is great on top of your favorite salad or as a dipping sauce for Fried Okra (page 95).

Curry "Chicken" Salad

GLUTEN-FREE, NUT-FREE, OIL-FREE, SOY-FREE

SERVES 4 TO 6 • PREP TIME: 30 MINUTES • COOK TIME: 20 MINUTES

FOR THE SALAD

2 (20-ounce) cans jackfruit in brine
½ cup diced celery
½ cup diced red onion
⅓ cup diced orange bell pepper

FOR THE DRESSING

¾ cup vegan mayo
1 teaspoon sea salt, or more to taste
Freshly ground black pepper
1 tablespoon minced garlic
1½ teaspoons curry powder
½ teaspoon turmeric
1 teaspoon granulated garlic
1 teaspoon white pepper
½ teaspoon onion powder
½ tablespoon agave nectar
½ teaspoon yellow mustard

This salad sells out every time I make it at my restaurant. Curry is not traditionally southern, but the bold spices and flavors come from the Caribbean, a region that greatly influenced soul food. Jackfruit is used as a chicken replacement in this recipe. I love cooking with jackfruit, because of the texture and meatiness and because it is so versatile. You can use roughly chopped Gardein vegan chicken strips instead of jackfruit for a faster alternative. For the mayo, I find that Just Mayo and Best Foods Vegan Mayo brands taste best.

1. Rinse and drain the jackfruit. Place the jackfruit pieces in a steamer and steam for 15 minutes; then remove and cool in the refrigerator for about 20 minutes.

2. While the jackfruit is cooling, in a medium mixing bowl, make the dressing by combining all the dressing ingredients in a medium mixing bowl and mixing well.

3. Once the jackfruit is fully cooled, place it on a cutting board and cut off and discard the hard core.

4. Combine the celery, onions, and bell peppers in a large mixing bowl. Add the cooked, chopped jackfruit and the dressing and stir to mix well.

....

Tip: Use a flour tortilla to make this into a delicious wrap, or use lettuce as a wrap for an even healthier version. Store leftovers in the refrigerator in a sealed container for 2 to 3 days.

Cajun Potato Salad

GLUTEN-FREE, NUT-FREE, SOY-FREE

SERVES 4 TO 6 • PREP TIME: 15 MINUTES • COOK TIME: 10 MINUTES, PLUS TIME TO COOL

Pinch sea salt

5 or 6 medium Yukon Gold potatoes, diced

¼ cup diced celery

¼ cup diced red onions

¼ cup diced red and green bell peppers

2 tablespoons diced dill pickles, with 1 tablespoon pickle juice reserved

3 green onions, chopped

2 teaspoons granulated garlic

2 tablespoons chopped fresh dill

¾ cup vegan mayo

1 teaspoon yellow mustard

½ tablespoon Creole Cajun Seasoning (page 123)

You can't even think about having southern barbecue without serving potato salad. This recipe was my nana's favorite side dish, and you could always find a fresh batch made for Sunday dinner. The Cajun seasoning adds just the right amount of heat to this traditional dish. For the vegan version, we simply switch to plant-based milk and vegan mayonnaise. This is great as a side dish or served on a bed of salad greens.

1. Fill a medium stockpot half full of water and bring to a boil. Add a pinch of salt.

2. Add the potatoes to the boiling water and cook until fork-tender, 8 to 10 minutes. Do not overcook.

3. Drain the potatoes, place them in a bowl, and set the bowl in the freezer for 5 to 8 minutes to cool.

4. Once the potatoes have cooled, take them out of the freezer and add the celery, red onions, bell peppers, pickles, green onions, garlic, and dill. Toss gently, then add the mayo, mustard, pickle juice, and Cajun seasoning and gently stir to combine.

Tip: Make the salad the day before to allow all the seasonings to really bloom.

Bacon-Lover Salad

GLUTEN-FREE, NUT-FREE, 30 MINUTES OR LESS

SERVES 4 TO 6 • PREP TIME: 15 MINUTES • COOK TIME: 15 MINUTES

FOR THE MARINADE

1½ tablespoons liquid smoke

¼ cup tamari

¼ cup maple syrup

FOR THE "BACON"

⅓ cup sweetened, shredded coconut flakes

½ cup chopped tempeh

FOR THE SALAD

2 pounds mixed salad greens

¼ cup diced onions

¼ cup shredded carrots

¼ cup shredded red cabbage

2 avocados, peeled and diced

¼ cup diced Roma tomatoes

½ cup avocado dressing (from the Avocado Slaw recipe, page 34)

Real bacon is a major heart-clogger, but who doesn't love the taste of bacon? The vegan version used in this dish provides a robust flavor and hearty texture that compare favorably to the real thing. King oyster mushrooms and sliced eggplant both work well as replacements for the tempeh if you are avoiding soy products.

1. Preheat the oven to 375°F. Line a baking pan with parchment paper.

2. In a small bowl, make the marinade by whisking together the marinade ingredients and set aside.

3. In a second small bowl, drizzle the coconut with half of the marinade and mix with a spoon until well combined.

4. In a third small bowl, pour the remaining marinade over the chopped tempeh and mix well. Allow to marinate for 5 minutes

5. Spread the tempeh on half of the baking pan, making a single layer.

6. Cut a 6-inch piece of aluminum foil and a 6-inch piece of parchment paper, then place the parchment on top of the foil to create a packet. Add the marinated coconut and fold the ends over to seal the packet.

7. Place the coconut packet on the baking pan next to the tempeh and bake for 6 to 8 minutes.

Continued

Bacon-Lover Salad *Continued*

8. While the "bacon" is baking, in a large salad bowl, arrange the salad ingredients. Pile the mixed greens on the bottom and then add the onions, carrots, cabbage, avocados, and tomatoes on top, lining them up side by side.

9. Remove the "bacon" from the oven. Top the salad with the tempeh bacon first, then sprinkle the coconut bacon over the entire salad. Drizzle with the avocado dressing and serve.

Three-Bean Salad

GLUTEN-FREE, NUT-FREE, SOY-FREE

SERVES 4 TO 6 • PREP TIME: 15 MINUTES, PLUS OVERNIGHT SOAKING • COOK TIME: 1 HOUR

FOR THE SALAD

½ cup dried black-eyed
   peas, soaked overnight

½ cup dried dark kidney
   beans, soaked overnight

½ cup dried chickpeas,
   soaked overnight

8 cups water

1 vegetable bouillon cube

½ cup diced onion

½ cup diced celery

⅓ cup diced green or red
   bell pepper

⅓ cup finely chopped
   broccoli

⅓ cup diced cucumber

FOR THE DRESSING

⅓ cup apple cider vinegar

2 tablespoons
   agave nectar

3 tablespoons grapeseed
   or sunflower oil

½ teaspoon finely chopped
   fresh thyme

½ teaspoon finely chopped
   fresh rosemary

½ teaspoon chopped
   fresh parsley

Sea salt

Pinch cayenne pepper

Beans, beans, good for your heart! This recipe is made with all the beans that are used in traditional soul food cooking. Soaking dried beans overnight cuts down the cooking time significantly and helps release the indigestible sugars that cause flatulence. Canned beans can be used in place of dried beans; just be sure to rinse them well before using.

1. In a stockpot over medium heat, combine the black-eyed peas, kidney beans, chickpeas, water, and bouillon cube.

2. Bring to a boil, then turn down the heat slightly and simmer for another 30 to 45 minutes, or until the beans are tender. When the beans are fully cooked, a fork should go right through them.

3. In a medium mixing bowl, make the dressing by whisking together all the dressing ingredients until well combined.

4. Drain the beans once they are fully cooked. Put the beans in a bowl and set in the freezer to cool for about 10 minutes.

5. Remove the beans from the freezer and combine them in a large bowl with the onion, celery, bell pepper, broccoli, and cucumber.

6. Pour the dressing over the bean salad and stir to mix well.

Barbecue Ranch Roasted Vegetable Salad

GLUTEN-FREE, NUT-FREE, 30 MINUTES OR LESS

SERVES 4 • PREP TIME: 15 MINUTES • COOK TIME: 15 MINUTES

FOR THE SALAD

1 cup large diced zucchini

1 cup large diced
    yellow squash

1 cup quartered
    Brussels sprouts

1 cup halved baby
    portobello mushrooms

2 tablespoons grapeseed
    or sunflower oil

FOR THE DRESSING

1 cup vegan mayo

¼ cup unsweetened
    plant-based milk

4 cloves garlic, minced

1½ teaspoons
    onion powder

1½ teaspoons dried dill

¼ teaspoon smoked paprika

¼ teaspoon sea salt

1 tablespoon dried parsley

1 tablespoon apple
    cider vinegar

¼ teaspoon freshly ground
    black pepper

¼ cup Peach-Habanero
    Barbecue Sauce
    (page 117)

This flavor combination is a surefire winner for almost everyone, especially children. When you're having a hard time getting the kids to eat their vegetables, making this recipe will put a stop to that.

1. Preheat the oven to 425°F. Line a baking pan with parchment paper.

2. In a large bowl, combine the zucchini, squash, Brussels sprouts, mushrooms, and oil and toss to mix.

3. Spread the vegetables evenly on the baking pan and roast for 10 to 12 minutes.

4. Meanwhile, in a medium bowl, make the dressing by whisking together all the dressing ingredients until well combined and set aside.

5. Remove the vegetables from the oven, place in a serving bowl, and drizzle with the dressing. Serve hot.

Tip: Use any vegetables that might already be in your refrigerator to save time and money. Store undressed, roasted vegetables in a sealed container in the refrigerator for 2 to 3 days.

Kale, Watermelon, and Apple Salad

GLUTEN-FREE, SOY-FREE, 30 MINUTES OR LESS

SERVES 4 • PREP TIME: 10 MINUTES

FOR THE DRESSING

3 tablespoons white balsamic vinegar

2 tablespoons grapeseed or sunflower oil

½ teaspoon agave nectar

½ teaspoon finely chopped fresh thyme

½ teaspoon sea salt, or more to taste

White pepper

FOR THE SALAD

1½ bunches lacinato kale, stemmed, and cut into thin ribbons

½ bunch dandelion greens, roughly chopped

10 basil leaves, roughly chopped

⅓ cup red cabbage

¼ cup thinly sliced onion

1 cup cubed ripe watermelon

1 cup peeled, diced apple

⅓ cup roasted cashews

This is a perfect summer salad that works well as either an entrée or a side dish. Watermelon is a traditional staple in southern food and grows bountifully in Georgia. I can remember my grandfather telling us stories about the reddest, most delicious watermelons they used to grow on their farm. I prefer Honeycrisp apples in this recipe, but you can use whatever is on hand.

1. In a medium bowl, make the dressing by whisking together all the dressing ingredients to combine.

2. In a large bowl or in individual serving bowls, build the salad beginning with a mound of kale and dandelion greens at the bottom; then the basil, cabbage, and onions; and finally the watermelon, apples, cashews, and a drizzle of dressing.

Cajun Corn Chowder, *page 45*

Chapter Four

Soups and Stews

Curry Sweet Potato and Kale Soup

GLUTEN-FREE, NUT-FREE, SOY-FREE

SERVES 4 TO 6 • PREP TIME: 10 MINUTES • COOK TIME: 30 MINUTES

2 tablespoons
  grapeseed oil
½ red onion, diced
4 tablespoons peeled,
  minced fresh ginger
2 garlic cloves, minced
Sea salt
2 medium sweet potatoes,
  peeled and diced
6 tablespoons red
  curry paste
1½ teaspoons turmeric
1 (13.5-ounce) can
  coconut cream
4 cups water
1 tablespoon agave nectar
4 cups roughly chopped
  kale leaves
⅓ cup frozen corn

Soups are a dish I could eat daily. Even during the brutal summertime here in Arizona, I still enjoy a hearty, yummy soup. Just not while outside. This soup brings together some popular soul food ingredients like kale, sweet potatoes, and corn and transforms them into liquid gold!

1. In a large stockpot over medium heat, heat the oil; then add the onions and ginger and sauté for 3 to 4 minutes, stirring frequently.

2. Add the garlic, salt to taste, sweet potatoes, curry paste, and turmeric, and stir. Cook for 2 to 3 minutes.

3. Add the coconut cream and water, stir, and bring to a slow simmer.

4. Simmer for about 15 minutes, or until the sweet potatoes are fork-tender; then add the agave nectar and simmer for another 5 minutes.

5. Add the kale and corn and stir. Taste for seasoning and add more salt if desired.

6. Cover, turn off the heat, and let sit for 5 minutes.

7. Serve alone or over cooked quinoa, rice, or your favorite grain.

Cajun Corn Chowder

NUT-FREE, SOY-FREE

SERVES 4 TO 6 • PREP TIME: 20 MINUTES • COOK TIME: 25 MINUTES

1 large green chile

1 red bell pepper

6 cups frozen corn, divided

2 cups coconut milk

1 vegetable bouillon cube

1 tablespoon grapeseed or sunflower oil

1½ medium red onions, diced

2 celery stalks, chopped

2 carrots, chopped

1 bay leaf

2 tablespoons garlic, minced

3 medium red potatoes, diced

½ teaspoon smoked paprika

2 teaspoons unbleached all-purpose flour

Sea salt

Freshly ground black pepper

2 cups water

¼ cup chopped fresh parsley

Chowders and stews are what I call stick-to-your-bones meals. This spicy, hearty, creamy bowl of deliciousness is packed with layers of flavors and textures.

1. To roast the peppers, turn a gas stove burner to medium heat. Place the green chile and the red bell pepper directly on top of the burner so that the fire starts to char the outside. Continue for 3 to 5 minutes, turning the peppers until all sides are charred.

2. Place the peppers in a small mixing bowl and tightly cover with plastic wrap, allowing the peppers to sweat for 5 to 10 minutes.

3. Uncover the bowl and peel the charred skin off the peppers. Cut off the tops and then seed and dice the peppers.

4. Place 3 cups of corn, the coconut milk, and the bouillon cube in a blender and blend until thick and creamy, 20 to 30 seconds. Pour the blended corn mixture into a bowl and set aside.

5. In a medium stockpot, heat the oil over medium-high heat. Once the oil is hot, add the onions, celery, carrots, and bay leaf and sauté for 4 to 5 minutes or until the onions are translucent.

6. Add the remaining 3 cups of corn and the garlic, potatoes, diced peppers, paprika, and flour, season with salt and black pepper, and stir.

Continued

Cajun Corn Chowder *Continued*

7. Add the water and corn purée and stir.

8. Allow the chowder to simmer on low heat for 15 to 20 minutes or until the potatoes are tender.

9. Remove the bay leaf and serve hot with a sprinkling of the parsley.

Tip: For a creamier soup, blend three-fourths of the corn with ¼ cup more water. For a thinner soup, add ½ cup of coconut milk and stir.

Detox Veggie Soup

GLUTEN-FREE, NUT-FREE, SOY-FREE

SERVES 6 • PREP TIME: 15 MINUTES • COOK TIME: 25 MINUTES

1 cup broccoli florets

1½ tablespoons grapeseed or sunflower oil, divided

Pinch sea salt

½ cup diced red onion

2½ teaspoons peeled and minced fresh ginger

3 garlic cloves, minced

1 cup chopped carrots

4 Roma tomatoes, diced

2 teaspoons dried thyme

1 teaspoon turmeric

¼ teaspoon cayenne pepper

Freshly ground black pepper

4 cups water

½ teaspoon liquid smoke

½ cup red cabbage

½ cup stemmed, chopped collards

1 tablespoon chopped fresh cilantro

Our bodies need detoxing from time to time. I try to do a detox every three months, and this soup is my go-to. Ginger is known for reducing inflammation and improving digestion, while cilantro assists in removing heavy metals from the body, and cayenne pepper helps purify the blood and burn fat.

1. Preheat the oven to 375°F. Line a baking pan with parchment paper.

2. In a small bowl, mix the broccoli florets, ½ tablespoon of oil, and the salt. Scatter the broccoli on the lined baking pan and bake for 5 minutes or until the broccoli tips are slightly charred. Remove from the oven and set aside to cool.

3. In a large stockpot, heat the remaining 1 tablespoon of oil on medium-high. Add the onions and ginger and sauté for 2 to 3 minutes. Add the garlic, carrots, tomatoes, thyme, turmeric, cayenne pepper, and black pepper and sauté until slightly softened.

4. Add the water and liquid smoke and bring to a slow boil.

5. Turn the heat down and allow to simmer for 5 to 10 minutes.

6. Remove from heat. Add the roasted broccoli, cabbage, and collards. Cover and let sit for 5 minutes, then serve topped with the cilantro.

Black-Eyed Peas with Okra and Greens

GLUTEN-FREE, NUT-FREE, SOY-FREE

SERVES 4 TO 6 • PREP TIME: 10 MINUTES • COOK TIME: 25 MINUTES

1½ tablespoons grapeseed or sunflower oil

1 cup diced red onions

½ cup diced red bell pepper

3 garlic cloves, minced

1 teaspoon dried thyme

1 teaspoon smoked paprika

1 teaspoon Creole Cajun Seasoning (page 123)

1 cup diced tomatoes

½ cup tomato sauce

Sea salt

Freshly ground black pepper, to taste

2 cups canned black-eyed peas, rinsed and drained

2 cups fresh okra

3½ cups water

2 cups stemmed, roughly chopped collards

2 cups stemmed, roughly chopped kale

¼ cup chopped fresh parsley, for garnish

"Prosperity Stew" is what I call this soup, as it's a remake of the stew my nana would make for every New Year's. In the African American community, black-eyed peas are a symbol of good luck and success. I really cannot recall too many times outside of the holidays that my family would eat black-eyed peas, and the holidays are mainly when I eat them now. Hopefully, this dish will bring you and your family as much prosperity and luck as I feel it has brought me and my family.

1. Heat the oil in a large stockpot over medium-high heat, then add the onions and bell peppers, stir, and cook for 2 to 3 minutes. Add the garlic, thyme, smoked paprika, Cajun seasoning, tomatoes, and tomato sauce, season with salt and black pepper, and stir. Cook for an additional 2 to 3 minutes.

2. Add the black-eyed peas, okra, and water. Bring to a boil, then turn down and simmer for 10 minutes. Add the collards and kale, stir, and simmer for another 5 minutes.

3. Turn the heat off, cover, and let sit for 5 minutes. Serve with a sprinkling of the parsley.

Tip: Serve with brown rice or quinoa and a side of corn cakes for a complete meal.

"Chicken" and Dumplings

NUT-FREE

SERVES 6 • PREP TIME: 10 MINUTES • COOK TIME: 40 MINUTES

FOR THE DUMPLINGS

2 cups unbleached
    all-purpose flour

2 teaspoons baking powder

½ teaspoon sea salt

2 tablespoons Earth
    Balance vegan butter

¾ cup plant-based milk

FOR THE STEW

3 tablespoons
    grapeseed oil

⅓ cup diced onions

3 celery stalks, chopped

2 carrots, chopped

1 teaspoon dried thyme

1 teaspoon rubbed sage

½ teaspoon onion powder

1 teaspoon dried
    rosemary, crushed

1 teaspoon salt

Freshly ground
    black pepper

½ teaspoon granulated
    garlic

½ teaspoon minced garlic

2 cups Gardein Chick'n
    Strips, chopped

½ cup frozen peas

1 bay leaf

This recipe is pure comfort food in a bowl. Not many people can make this dish like my aunt did growing up. My vegan version has fluffy pillow dumplings along with savory earthy herbs and "chicken." It makes my mouth and stomach joyous!

1. Line a baking pan with parchment paper.

2. To make the dumplings, in a large mixing bowl, place the flour, baking powder, salt, butter, and milk. Using a handheld electric mixer, mix until well incorporated and the batter is nice and thick.

3. Scoop up large spoonfuls of batter and gently form small balls with your hands. Set the dumplings on the lined baking pan. Continue until the batter is gone.

4. To make the stew, heat the oil in a large stockpot over medium-heat, then add the onions, celery, carrots, thyme, sage, onion powder, rosemary, salt, pepper, and granulated garlic. Cook for 2 to 3 minutes, stirring occasionally.

5. Add the minced garlic, Chick'n Strips, peas, and bay leaf and stir. Cook for another 2 to 3 minutes, then add the flour and stir until well combined. Add the vegetable stock and stir to blend well.

6. As the mixture begins to thicken, allow it to come to a soft boil. Add the dumplings one at a time. Stir frequently and cook for 20 to 25 minutes.

Continued

½ cup unbleached
    all-purpose flour
5 cups vegetable stock
Pinch dried parsley

7. Take a dumpling out of the stew to test the doneness. With a spoon, break off a piece of the dumpling, making sure to get a piece from the middle. It should be soft all the way through. If the dumplings are hard in the middle, lower the heat and simmer for another 5 minutes. Remove the bay leaf.

8. Serve in bowls with the parsley sprinkled on top.

Tip: For a gluten-free version, use gluten-free flour and try shredded cooked jackfruit for the mock "chicken" for almost the exact same texture and flavor profile as traditional chicken and dumplings.

West African Peanut Stew

GLUTEN-FREE, SOY-FREE, 30 MINUTES OR LESS

SERVES 6 • PREP TIME: 5 MINUTES • COOK TIME: 20 MINUTES

2 tablespoons
    grapeseed oil
1 cup diced onion
1 teaspoon peeled and
    minced fresh ginger
4 cloves garlic, minced
1½ cups peeled and diced
    sweet potatoes
1 teaspoon cumin
Sea salt
1 habanero pepper
2 vegetable bouillon cubes
4 cups warm water
¾ cup chunky
    peanut butter
1½ teaspoons sriracha
    (optional)
1 (6-ounce) can
    tomato paste
1 bunch collard greens,
    stemmed and
    roughly chopped
½ cup frozen corn
¼ cup peanuts,
    roughly chopped
¼ cup roughly chopped
    fresh parsley

This is a traditional West African stew that's packed with protein and flavor. The creaminess from the peanut butter and textures from the veggies make this one of my favorite soups. If you're a peanut butter fan like me, you're going to love this hearty stew. Serve it over brown rice or quinoa for an even heartier meal.

1. In a medium stockpot, heat the oil over medium-high heat, then add the onions and ginger and sauté for 2 to 3 minutes. Add the garlic, stir, and sauté for another 1 to 2 minutes.

2. Add the sweet potatoes, cumin, salt to taste, and whole habanero pepper and sauté for another 4 to 5 minutes.

3. Meanwhile, add the bouillon cubes to the warm water and stir to dissolve.

4. Add the dissolved bouillon, peanut butter, sriracha (if using), and tomato paste to the stockpot, and stir to combine. Cover, bring to a soft boil, and then turn the heat to low and allow to simmer.

5. Add the greens and corn and simmer for another 5 to 10 minutes or until the sweet potatoes and collards are soft. Remove the habanero and discard.

6. Serve in bowls topped with the chopped peanuts and fresh parsley.

Three-Bean Chili

GLUTEN-FREE, NUT-FREE, SOY-FREE

SERVES 6 • PREP TIME: 10 MINUTES • COOK TIME: 30 MINUTES

2 tablespoons
   grapeseed oil

1 cup diced onion

½ cup diced red or green
   bell pepper

4 garlic cloves, minced

1¾ cups water

1 cup frozen
   black-eyed peas

1 cup canned kidney
   beans, rinsed
   and drained

1 cup frozen butter beans

1 cup frozen corn

5 tablespoons
   tomato paste

1 (28-ounce) can diced
   tomatoes

2 teaspoons cumin

1 teaspoon sea salt

1 teaspoon onion powder

2 teaspoons chili powder

1 teaspoon
   smoked paprika

1 teaspoon liquid smoke

¼ teaspoon freshly ground
   black pepper

Chili is a southern recipe that originated in northern Mexico and Texas, and it is something I made quite often when my sons were growing up. I knew my sons could use the leftovers to make things like chili-and-cheese quesadillas, burritos, or nachos. I love to use Chao vegan cheese as a topping because it melts amazingly.

1. In a large stockpot, heat the oil over medium-high heat, add the onion and bell peppers, and sauté for 5 minutes. Add the garlic and sauté for another 1 to 2 minutes, stirring to avoid burning the garlic.

2. Add the water, then stir in the black-eyed peas, kidney beans, butter beans, corn, tomato paste, diced tomatoes, cumin, salt, onion powder, chili powder, smoked paprika, liquid smoke, and black pepper. Bring to a boil, then simmer for another 20 to 25 minutes.

Tip: For more protein and texture, add 1½ cups of presoaked TVP or crumbled vegan sausage.

Jackfruit Gumbo

NUT-FREE

SERVES 4 TO 6 • PREP TIME: 15 MINUTES • COOK TIME: 30 MINUTES

1 (20-ounce) can young
    jackfruit in brine
1 vegetable bouillon cube
4 cups warm water
1 (12.9-ounce) package
    Field Roast Smoked
    Apple Sage Sausage
1½ tablespoons grapeseed
    or sunflower oil
1½ cups diced onion
1 cup diced yellow
    bell pepper
3 celery stalks, chopped
2 carrots, chopped
2 tablespoons unbleached
    all-purpose flour
6 garlic cloves, minced
½ cup diced tomatoes
1 cup puréed tomatoes
2 to 3 teaspoons Creole
    Cajun Seasoning
    (page 123)
½ teaspoon cumin
1 teaspoon sea salt
Freshly ground
    black pepper
1½ cups canned
    kidney beans, rinsed
    and drained
½ cup frozen corn
2½ cups fresh or frozen okra

Traditionally, gumbo has sausage, shrimp, or chicken to get a smoky and meaty texture. Here jackfruit is used as a chicken replacement along with a delicious apple-sage sausage to give you the comforting dish you are looking for.

1. Drain and rinse the jackfruit.

2. On a cutting board, remove the core from the jackfruit and discard, then use a potato masher to mash the jackfruit until it resembles pulled meat. Place the mashed jackfruit in a bowl and set aside.

3. In a medium bowl, combine the bouillon cube and the warm water, stir, and set aside.

4. Cut the vegan sausage in half and slice about ½ inch thick.

5. In a large stockpot, heat the oil over medium-high heat, then add the sausage, onion, bell peppers, celery, and carrots. Sauté for 3 to 5 minutes, stirring often. Once the mixture is fragrant, add the flour and stir until the flour is light brown. Then add the garlic and cook for 1 minute.

6. Add the diced tomatoes, puréed tomatoes, bouillon water, jackfruit, Cajun seasoning, cumin, salt, and black pepper and stir. Cook for 3 to 5 minutes.

7. Add the beans, corn, and okra and cook for another 15 to 20 minutes. If the stew becomes too thick, add ½ to 1 cup of water to reach the desired thickness. Serve hot.

Loaded Potato Soup

GLUTEN-FREE, NUT-FREE, SOY-FREE, 30 MINUTES OR LESS

SERVES 4 TO 6 • PREP TIME: 10 MINUTES • COOK TIME: 20 MINUTES

FOR THE SOUP

1 tablespoon plus
    1 teaspoon grapeseed oil

1 small onion, diced

4 garlic cloves, minced

1 vegetable bouillon cube,
    dissolved in 5 cups
    warm water

1 bay leaf

4 russet potatoes, peeled
    and diced

¼ teaspoon smoked
    paprika

½ teaspoon dried thyme

½ teaspoon dried crushed
    rosemary

Sea salt

Freshly ground black pepper

⅓ cup nutritional yeast

1 can full-fat coconut milk

FOR THE TOPPING

2 cups broccoli florets

½ cup corn

¼ cup diced red bell pepper

2 teaspoons sunflower oil

Pinch salt

This quick and easy soup is creamy and chunky and has amazing flavor. Even though this is not a traditional soul food dish, it's high on the comfort food list. One bowl of this soup will have your belly happy and full for hours. Top with leftover cornbread chopped into small cubes and warmed in the oven to add a southern flair to this recipe.

1. Preheat the oven to 450°F. Line a baking pan with parchment paper.

2. In a large stockpot, heat the oil over medium-high heat, then add the onions and sauté for 2 to 3 minutes. Add the garlic and sauté for another 1 to 2 minutes.

3. Add the bouillon water, bay leaf, potatoes, smoked paprika, thyme, and rosemary. Season with salt and pepper.

4. Stir and cook until the potatoes are fork-tender, 10 to 15 minutes, then add the nutritional yeast, turn off the heat, and add the coconut milk. Remove the bay leaf.

5. To make the topping, in a medium bowl, toss the broccoli florets, corn, and bell peppers with the oil and salt. Scatter the veggie mixture on the lined baking pan and roast for 5 minutes or until the tips are slightly charred. Remove from the oven and cover to keep warm.

½ cup **Smoky Tempeh Bacon (page 17) or coconut bacon (from the Bacon-Lover Salad recipe, page 37) (optional)**

¼ cup **chopped chives (optional)**

6. Using an immersion blender, blend the soup until it is mostly smooth. I prefer to keep some chunks of potato, so I usually blend for only 1 to 2 minutes. Blend longer for a smoother texture.

7. Serve in soup bowls and top with the roasted vegetables and additional toppings as desired.

"Chicken" Noodle Soup

NUT-FREE

SERVES 4 • PREP TIME: 5 MINUTES • COOK TIME: 30 MINUTES

2 tablespoons grapeseed
    or sunflower oil, divided
1 (10-ounce) bag Gardein
    Chick'n Strips,
    roughly chopped
4 celery stalks, chopped
2 medium carrots, chopped
1½ cups diced onion
½ teaspoon dried crushed
    rosemary
½ teaspoon dried thyme
Sea salt
Freshly ground
    black pepper
3 cloves garlic, minced
1 cup dried noodles
2 vegetable bouillon
    cubes, dissolved in
    6 cups water

Even though this dish is considered an American classic, to me it encompasses what soul food is all about: a few simple ingredients that are transformed through love into a soulful dish. Whenever I wasn't feeling well, my nana would make this, and it always made me feel better.

1. In a medium stockpot, heat 1 tablespoon of oil over medium-high heat, then add the Chick'n Strips and cook until browned on both sides, 3 to 4 minutes on each side. Remove from the oil, place on a paper towel–lined plate, and set aside.

2. Immediately add the celery, carrots, onion, rosemary, and thyme to the hot oil and sauté for 3 to 5 minutes. Season with salt and pepper.

3. Once the vegetables are slightly soft, add the garlic and sauté for 1 to 2 minutes, stirring to avoid burning.

4. In a small pot on another burner, bring a generous amount of water and a pinch of salt to a boil. Add the dried noodles, stir, and cook for 4 to 5 minutes or until the pasta is slightly more than al dente. Drain, drizzle the noodles with the remaining 1 tablespoon of oil, toss to coat, and set aside.

5. Add the bouillon water and chick'n to the veggies, bring to a soft boil, and then turn the heat to low and simmer for 15 minutes.

6. Remove from the heat and add the noodles.

Caribbean Coconut
Greens, *page 62*

Chapter Five
Appetizers and Sides

Loaded Plantain Bites

NUT-FREE, SOY-FREE, 30 MINUTES OR LESS

SERVES 4 TO 6 • PREP TIME: 10 MINUTES • COOK TIME: 10 MINUTES

4 ripe plantains

Coconut oil or spray

1 cup Three-Bean Salad (page 39)

1 ripe avocado, peeled and diced

Crispy onions (from the Heirloom Tomato and Avocado Stacks recipe, page 31)

This sweet and savory appetizer is a real crowd-pleaser. Hosting an office party or a casual summer get-together? This dish is sure to be the talk of the town! Plantains are not only tasty but also easily digested, rich in fiber, and high in potassium and vitamins A, C, and B$_6$. This recipe relies on the Three-Bean Salad from chapter 3 (page 39), but if you don't have any on hand, try using black beans. It's also great topped with Smoky Tempeh Bacon crumbles (page 17).

1. Preheat the oven to 400°F. Line a baking pan with parchment paper.

2. Cut the tops and bottoms off the plantains, then gently slice the skin from top to bottom, peel, and slice the fruit into 2-inch diagonal slices.

3. Place the plantain slices on the lined baking pan and brush or spray with the coconut oil.

4. Bake for 3 to 4 minutes (until golden brown on one side), then flip the plantains and bake for another 3 to 4 minutes. Remove from the oven and let cool for 2 to 3 minutes.

5. Place the baked plantain slices on a serving tray, and top each with 1 tablespoon of the Three-Bean Salad, diced avocado, and Crispy Onions.

Butternut Squash Mac 'n' "Cheese"

NUT-FREE, SOY-FREE

SERVES 6 • PREP TIME: 15 MINUTES • COOK TIME: 20 MINUTES

2 cups peeled and diced
    butternut squash

½ large onion, diced

1 (12-ounce) package
    macaroni noodles

1 tablespoon sunflower oil

6 tablespoons
    nutritional yeast

2 teaspoons lemon or
    lime juice

1 teaspoon salt

½ teaspoon
    yellow mustard

1 teaspoon
    granulated garlic

Pinch freshly ground
    black pepper

½ teaspoon
    smoked paprika

½ teaspoon turmeric

½ teaspoon dried sage

½ teaspoon liquid smoke

Mac 'n' cheese is truly a staple in southern cuisine, and as most of us know, traditional southern recipes often call for tons of butter and milk. Over the years I've developed several plant-based mac 'n' cheese recipes, and this is my favorite. The creaminess of the squash and flavor punch of the seasonings are not only approved by me, they are also kid-approved.

1. In a medium pot, combine the butternut squash and onion and cover with water by at least an inch or two. Bring to a boil, reduce the heat to medium, and simmer until the vegetables are tender, about 15 minutes.

2. Meanwhile, cook the macaroni noodles according to the package directions, drain, drizzle with the oil, and stir. Return the cooked noodles to the pot used to cook them and set aside.

3. When the squash and onions are tender, drain them, reserving ¼ cup of the liquid. In a high-speed blender, combine the squash, onions, nutritional yeast, lemon juice, salt, mustard, granulated garlic, black pepper, smoked paprika, turmeric, sage, liquid smoke, and reserved cooking liquid from the squash. Blend until completely smooth.

4. Add the butternut squash sauce to the macaroni noodles and stir, making sure every noodle is covered in sauce. Warm through if needed.

Caribbean Coconut Greens

GLUTEN-FREE, NUT-FREE, SOY-FREE

SERVES 6 • PREP TIME: 15 MINUTES • COOK TIME: 20 MINUTES

2 tablespoons grapeseed
  or sunflower oil

½ medium onion, diced

2 teaspoons dried thyme

1 teaspoon liquid smoke

3 teaspoons
  granulated garlic

Sea salt

Freshly ground
  black pepper

3 bunches kale, stemmed
  and roughly chopped

1 (13.5-ounce) can
  coconut cream

2 cups water

½ cup shredded carrots
  (optional)

½ cup finely shredded red
  cabbage (optional)

My nana's greens would melt in your mouth. She cooked them for hours along with smoked turkey necks. This recipe is my healthy, quick, but still delicious version of my nana's greens. Instead of smoked meats, I use liquid smoke to give these greens the perfect amount of smokiness. The addition of the coconut cream and thyme gives this dish a Caribbean flair.

1. In a medium stockpot, heat the oil over medium heat.

2. Add the onion, stir, and sauté for 3 to 4 minutes. Add the thyme, liquid smoke, and granulated garlic, season with salt and pepper, and stir. Reduce the heat to low, and simmer for 3 to 4 minutes.

3. Once the onions are translucent and their aroma fills the air, add the kale. Give it a quick stir, cover, and simmer on low for another 4 to 5 minutes or until the kale is soft.

4. While the kale is cooking down, in a small bowl, whisk the coconut cream and water together.

5. After the kale has softened, add the coconut cream mixture to it and cook for another 5 to 7 minutes. Remove from the heat, uncover, and stir to mix well.

6. Top with the shredded carrots and red cabbage (if using).

Tip: Collard greens, Swiss chard, and most other greens can be substituted for the kale. Collards require an additional 5 minutes of cooking.

Cajun Crabless Jackfruit Balls

NUT-FREE, SOY-FREE

SERVES 6 · PREP TIME: 45 MINUTES TO 1 HOUR 15 MINUTES · COOK TIME: 10 MINUTES

1 (20-ounce) can young jackfruit in brine

2 tablespoons flax meal

6 tablespoons warm water

1 cup vegan mayo

½ teaspoon onion powder

1 teaspoon mustard

1 teaspoon Old Bay seasoning

1 teaspoon Creole Cajun Seasoning (page 123)

1 teaspoon granulated garlic

1 teaspoon vegan Worcestershire sauce

½ teaspoon freshly ground black pepper

½ red onion, diced

½ cup diced red bell pepper

1 tablespoon lemon juice

½ cup bread crumbs or crumbled saltine crackers

1 to 2 tablespoons grapeseed oil

½ cup panko bread crumbs

Tartar Sauce, for dipping sauce (optional, page 121)

Cajun Chipotle Aioli, for dipping sauce (optional, page 126)

Jackfruit is wonderfully versatile and just plain fun to transform in vegan cooking. This unripe fruit can be used as a chicken, crab, or pork replacement. In this recipe, I don't remove the cores from the jackfruit in order to recreate the texture of lump crab meat. If you prefer more of a shredded texture, remove the core and mash the jackfruit until it is shredded.

1. Drain the jackfruit. Rinse well and pat dry with paper towels. Chop the jackfruit into pieces resembling lump crab meat, then place in a medium mixing bowl and set aside.

2. To make a flax egg, combine the flax meal and warm water in a small bowl, stir, and set aside for at least 5 minutes.

3. In another bowl, combine the vegan mayo, flax egg, onion powder, mustard, Old Bay, Cajun seasoning, granulated garlic, Worcestershire, and black pepper.

4. Add the mayo mixture, onion, bell pepper, and lemon juice to the jackfruit, then add the bread crumbs and stir to mix well.

5. Cover the bowl and place in the refrigerator for 1 hour or the freezer for 30 minutes.

6. In a skillet, heat the oil over medium-high heat.

Continued

Cajun Crabless Jackfruit Balls *Continued*

7. Remove the jackfruit mixture from the refrigerator or freezer. Form medium balls with your hands, roll individual jackfruit balls in the panko bread crumbs, and then place in the skillet and fry until golden brown, 5 to 10 minutes, turning to brown on all sides.

8. Remove the browned jackfruit balls and place on a paper towel–lined plate to drain off excess oil. Serve with the vegan tartar sauce or aioli dipping sauce.

Tip: Store premade balls/patties for 30 days in the freezer or up to 3 days in the refrigerator.

Caribbean Johnny Cakes

NUT-FREE

SERVES 4 TO 6 • PREP TIME: 45 MINUTES TO 1 HOUR 15 MINUTES • COOK TIME: 10 MINUTES

3 cups unbleached
    all-purpose flour, plus
    more for kneading

1 tablespoon
    baking powder

3 tablespoons cane sugar

1 teaspoon sea salt

1½ tablespoons Earth
    Balance vegan butter, at
    room temperature

1 cup water

Coconut oil spray

1 cup grapeseed oil,
    for frying

Johnny cakes are a staple side dish in Caribbean cooking. These johnny cakes are a variation of the fry bread that is traditionally paired with stews or barbecue dishes. Slice them open and fill them with Jerk Barbecue-Pulled Mushrooms (page 99) for a creative, delicious sandwich.

1. In a medium bowl, combine 3 cups of flour with the baking powder, sugar, and salt, then cut in the butter with a pastry cutter or two forks and mix well using your hands.

2. Slowly add the water and continue to mix until smooth and well combined.

3. On a dry surface, sprinkle some flour. Transfer the dough mixture to the floured surface and knead for 3 to 5 minutes, or until the dough is elastic and smooth.

4. Coat a medium bowl with coconut oil spray and place the dough in the bowl. Cover with plastic wrap and allow the dough to rest for 30 minutes to 1 hour.

5. In a medium stockpot, heat the oil over medium heat.

6. While the oil is heating, uncover the dough and begin to make golf ball–size balls (2 to 3 ounces of dough each). Once all the balls are formed, roll them out on the floured surface, making circles and then using the palm of your hand to gently press each one to about 1-inch thickness.

Continued

Caribbean Johnny Cakes *Continued*

7. Use a fork to poke holes in each piece of dough.

8. Gently place the dough pieces one at a time in the hot oil and fry until golden brown, 2 to 3 minutes on each side.

9. Remove from the oil, drain on paper towels or paper bags, and serve with your favorite soup or dish.

Hush Puppies

SOY-FREE, 30 MINUTES OR LESS

SERVES 4 TO 6 • PREP TIME: 5 MINUTES • COOK TIME: 15 MINUTES

1½ cups cornmeal

½ cup unbleached
all-purpose flour

½ teaspoon salt

½ teaspoon baking powder

1 small onion, chopped

½ cup corn kernels

½ jalapeño, diced

1 teaspoon cane sugar

1 cup unsweetened
almond milk

1 tablespoon grapeseed
oil, plus 2 cups for frying

Hush puppies are perfect little fried cornbread balls. I created this recipe especially for my sons when they were younger. Most Fridays I would serve fried fish and hush puppies. Now, I serve these with my Fishless Banana-Blossom Fish (page 98). The crunchy outside and fluffy center make these a delicious side to any meal.

1. Combine all the ingredients except the oil for frying in a medium bowl and whisk to mix well.

2. In a medium pot, heat the frying oil over medium heat.

3. Once the oil is hot, carefully drop a spoonful of batter at a time into the oil.

4. Turn the hush puppies so that they brown on all sides, 1-2 minutes on each side.

5. Once the hush puppies have browned, remove them from the oil and drain on paper towels or a paper bag.

Crispy Avocado Fries

GLUTEN-FREE, NUT-FREE, 30 MINUTES OR LESS

SERVES 4 TO 6 • PREP TIME: 10 MINUTES • COOK TIME: 15 MINUTES

½ cup gluten-free flour

½ teaspoon onion powder

½ teaspoon
    granulated garlic

½ teaspoon
    smoked paprika

½ teaspoon sea salt

½ teaspoon dried parsley

⅓ cup plant-based milk

1½ cups gluten-free
    panko bread crumbs
    or crushed gluten-free
    cornflakes

4 large or 6 or 7 small
    avocados

Coconut oil spray

⅓ cup Vegan Ranch (from
    the Barbecue Ranch
    Roasted Vegetable
    Salad recipe, page 40)

Avocado has earned its place on the list of my top five favorite fruits not only for its nutrient profile but because its versatility is amazing. Avocado can be used in desserts, salads, spreads, sauces, or as a yummy burger topping. These fries are yet another example of just how many ways you can transform this ingredient. Crispy on the outside and creamy on the inside, these fries are great toppers for burgers, salads, or Butternut Squash Mac 'n' "Cheese" (page 61). If you love avocado like I do, you'll have this recipe memorized in no time from making it so much.

1. Preheat the oven to 425°F. Line a baking pan with parchment paper.

2. In a medium mixing bowl, combine the flour, onion powder, granulated garlic, paprika, salt, dried parsley, and milk and whisk until well combined.

3. Pour the panko bread crumbs into a shallow dish. Arrange the wet mix bowl, the breading dish, and the lined baking pan in a row.

4. Slice the avocados in half, remove the seed, and then cut each half into 4 to 6 slices.

5. With a spoon, scoop the slices out of the peel. Dip each slice into the wet batter, shake off any excess wet mix, and then place in the breading, turning and gently pressing until fully coated.

6. Place the coated slices one at a time on the lined baking pan. Repeat until all the slices are coated. Spray each slice lightly with coconut oil.

7. Bake for 5 to 6 minutes on each side, until golden brown and crispy, turning halfway through the baking process.

8. Remove from the oven and allow to cool for 3 to 4 minutes.

9. Serve with the Vegan Ranch.

Tip: Try pan- or air-frying as an alternative to baking. Store any leftovers in the refrigerator in an airtight container for 2 to 3 days, and reheat in the oven at 400°F for 5 minutes or using a skillet coated with oil or spray.

Candied Yams

GLUTEN-FREE, NUT-FREE

SERVES 4 TO 6 • PREP TIME: 15 MINUTES • COOK TIME: 1 HOUR 5 MINUTES

4 medium sweet potatoes

Nonstick cooking spray

¼ cup coconut sugar

½ teaspoon ground ginger

1 cup pineapple juice

1 cup crushed pineapple

½ cup maple syrup or
    agave nectar

2 teaspoons vanilla extract

1½ teaspoons cinnamon

¼ teaspoon salt

4 tablespoons (½ stick)
    Earth Balance
    vegan butter

Our family Sunday dinners always included certain staples, and candied yams were one of them. Traditionally, this dish is made with lots of butter, sugar, and syrup and topped with toasted marshmallows. I always felt like this dish was more of a super-sweet dessert than a side. My recipe uses coconut sugar and maple syrup, two natural sweeteners that do not spike sugar levels. These candied yams are perfectly sweet, with a hint of citrus to balance the flavors and marry them together.

1. Preheat the oven to 375°F. Peel the sweet potatoes and cut into ¼-inch round slices.

2. Lightly spray a 9-by-13-inch baking dish with cooking spray, then arrange the slices in the baking dish.

3. In a medium mixing bowl, combine the sugar, ginger, pineapple juice, and pineapple, then stir in the maple syrup, vanilla, cinnamon, and salt.

4. Pour this mixture evenly over the sweet potatoes, then add the butter in dollops around the baking dish. Cover with parchment paper and then aluminum foil, and bake for 45 minutes.

5. Remove the foil and parchment paper, baste the sweet potatoes with the liquid in the baking dish, and bake for an additional 20 minutes uncovered.

Garlic-Smashed Potatoes

GLUTEN-FREE, NUT-FREE

SERVES 4 TO 6 • PREP TIME: 10 MINUTES • COOK TIME: 30 MINUTES

Coconut oil spray

1½ pounds red or purple potatoes

2 tablespoons Earth Balance vegan butter, melted

3 cloves garlic, minced

1 teaspoon crushed rosemary

Sea salt

1 tablespoon nutritional yeast

Freshly ground black pepper

These crispy, buttery potatoes taste amazing on their own and are also fun to use as a base for loaded potato bites, a great dish to serve at a party or family get-together. Add Jerk Barbecue-Pulled Mushrooms (page 99) and vegan cheese, chives, vegan sour cream and bacon, or any of your favorite toppings.

1. Preheat the oven to 400°F. Coat a baking pan with coconut oil spray.

2. Wash the potatoes. Place the potatoes in a medium stockpot, cover with salted water, and bring to a boil. Cover the pot and cook the potatoes until fork-tender, 15 to 20 minutes, then drain.

3. While the potatoes are cooking, combine the melted butter, garlic, rosemary, and salt to taste in a small mixing bowl and set aside.

4. Place the potatoes on the coated baking pan, then use a potato masher to gently smash each potato (do not fully smash).

5. Using a pastry brush, coat each smashed potato with the butter mixture, then sprinkle the nutritional yeast and pepper to taste on top. Lightly spray each potato with coconut oil spray, then bake for 7 to 10 minutes, or until the edges are browned and crispy.

Zucchini and Eggplant Fries

NUT-FREE, OIL-FREE, SOY-FREE, 30 MINUTES OR LESS

SERVES 4 TO 6 • PREP TIME: 10 MINUTES • COOK TIME: 20 MINUTES

½ cup unbleached
    all-purpose flour

½ teaspoon sea salt

½ teaspoon
    granulated garlic

½ teaspoon dried parsley

½ teaspoon onion powder

½ teaspoon oregano

Pinch cayenne pepper

¼ cup nutritional yeast

½ cup water or
    plant-based milk

2 cups panko bread
    crumbs or crushed
    cornflakes

1 medium eggplant

2 medium zucchini

Eggplant is a favorite of mine. Fun fact: Since this nightshade has seeds, it is technically classified as a fruit or berry. These fries are healthy, filling, quick, delicious, and a perfect alternative to the carb overload you often feel with fried potatoes. I love to dip these in Vegan Ranch (from the Barbecue Ranch Roasted Vegetable Salad recipe, page 40) or Peach-Habanero Barbecue Sauce (page 117).

1. Preheat the oven to 425°F. Line a baking pan with parchment paper.

2. In a medium mixing bowl, whisk together the flour, salt, granulated garlic, parsley, onion powder, oregano, cayenne pepper, nutritional yeast, and water.

3. Pour the panko bread crumbs into a shallow dish. Line up the wet mix, the dry mix, and the lined baking pan on the countertop.

4. Slice the eggplant and the zucchini into thick fry slices. One at a time, dip each slice into the wet mix, shake off any excess, and then roll in the dry mix until fully coated. Place each coated fry on the lined baking pan and continue until all the fries are fully dredged.

5. Bake for 20 minutes or until crispy and golden brown.

Tip: Not a big eggplant fan? Try using another vegetable, like yellow or Mexican squash.

Polenta with Barbecue-Pulled Mushrooms

GLUTEN-FREE, NUT-FREE, SOY-FREE

SERVES 4 TO 6 • PREP TIME: 30 MINUTES • COOK TIME: 10 MINUTES

2½ cups water

½ cup coconut milk

Pinch freshly ground
    black pepper

1½ teaspoons
    minced garlic

½ teaspoon crushed dried
    rosemary

½ teaspoon onion powder

½ teaspoon sea salt

1 cup coarse cornmeal

Coconut oil spray

3 tablespoons
    grapeseed oil

Jerk Barbecue-Pulled
    Mushrooms (page 99)

Polenta has a texture similar to grits and works well in many soul food dishes. Try adding different seasoning blends or fresh herbs, or top with vegan sausage crumbles and a little gravy.

1. Preheat the oven to 450°F. Line a baking pan with parchment paper and set aside.

2. In a medium stockpot, combine the water, coconut milk, black pepper, garlic, rosemary, onion powder, and salt. Bring to a gentle boil, then reduce the heat slightly. Slowly add in the cornmeal, stirring constantly to prevent lumping.

3. Turn the heat to low and simmer, stirring frequently, until thick, about 10 minutes.

4. Spread the cooked polenta on the lined baking pan to form a ½-inch-thick layer, and let cool completely.

5. Coat the inside of a small glass jar lid with coconut oil spray, and use the lid to cut out circles of the cooled polenta.

6. Heat 1 tablespoon of oil in a nonstick pan. Place the polenta circles in the hot oil and cook for 1 to 2 minutes on each side, until golden brown. Continue this process until all the circles have been browned, replenishing the oil as needed. Place the browned polenta on a paper bag and allow to drain.

7. Top individual circles with the Jerk Barbecue-Pulled Mushrooms and serve.

Fried Cabbage

GLUTEN-FREE, NUT-FREE, 30 MINUTES OR LESS

SERVES 4 TO 6 • PREP TIME: 10 MINUTES • COOK TIME: 15 MINUTES

2 tablespoons
    grapeseed oil

1 medium red onion, diced

½ teaspoon dried thyme

3 cloves garlic, minced

1 medium head
    cabbage, chopped

1 teaspoon Creole Cajun
    Seasoning (page 123)

¼ teaspoon
    smoked paprika

½ teaspoon onion powder

½ teaspoon
    granulated garlic

Pinch cayenne pepper

1 tablespoon vegan butter

⅓ cup water

½ teaspoon liquid smoke

Fried buttery cabbage is a dish that was on the table at every family holiday meal during my childhood. The traditional recipe is cooked with bacon fat to give the cabbage a smoky flavor. This recipe doesn't use bacon fat, but it will not disappoint! It's packed with flavor and has a nice hint of smokiness.

1. In a large skillet, heat the oil over medium heat. Add the onion and thyme and cook for 2 to 3 minutes. Add the minced garlic, stir, and cook for another minute. Do not allow the garlic to burn.

2. Stir in the cabbage, Cajun seasoning, smoked paprika, onion powder, granulated garlic, and cayenne pepper. Cook for 1 to 2 minutes.

3. Add the butter, water, and liquid smoke and cook for 8 to 10 minutes, stirring occasionally.

4. Serve hot.

Tip: Serve with cornbread and black-eyed peas or with Barbecue Riblets (page 107).

Island-Style Rice and Beans

GLUTEN-FREE, NUT-FREE, SOY-FREE, 30 MINUTES OR LESS

SERVES 6 • PREP TIME: 5 MINUTES • COOK TIME: 25 MINUTES

2 cups long-grain rice

¼ cup grapeseed or
sunflower oil

1 medium onion, diced

3 garlic cloves, minced

2 sprigs fresh thyme
or 1½ teaspoons
dried thyme

1 Scotch bonnet pepper

1 (13.5-ounce) can red
kidney beans, drained
and rinsed

1 (13.5-ounce) can
coconut cream

2 bay leaves

2 teaspoons Creole Cajun
Seasoning (page 123)

1 teaspoon
smoked paprika

Sea salt

3 cups water

When I was around 12 years old, my sisters, my three cousins, and I all stayed with my father for the summer. I swear we had rice and beans so many different ways for breakfast, lunch, and dinner that I never wanted to eat this dish again! It was some years before I did eat rice and beans again, and when I did, I realized that I really do love a good flavorful bowl of rice and beans, either thanks to—or in spite of—my father.

1. Rinse the rice until the water runs clear.

2. Heat the oil in a medium saucepan over medium heat, then add the onions, garlic, thyme, and whole Scotch bonnet pepper. Sauté for 1 to 2 minutes.

3. Stir the rice and the beans into the pan and cook for another 2 minutes, then add the coconut cream, the bay leaves, the Cajun seasoning, the paprika, a pinch or two of salt, and the water. Bring to a boil, reduce the heat, cover, and simmer until the rice is cooked, about 20 minutes. Stir occasionally to keep the bottom from sticking or burning.

4. Remove the Scotch bonnet pepper, bay leaves, and thyme sprigs before serving.

Tip: This recipe works well with black beans and chickpeas if you don't have kidney beans or don't care for them. If you have leftovers, use them to make a flavorful burrito or add them to your favorite salad. Store refrigerated in a sealed container for up to 3 days.

Green Beans with Shallots and Mushrooms

GLUTEN-FREE, NUT-FREE, SOY-FREE, 30 MINUTES OR LESS

SERVES 6 • PREP TIME: 5 MINUTES • COOK TIME: 15 MINUTES

1 teaspoon sea salt, plus
more to taste

1 pound fresh green beans,
washed and trimmed

2 tablespoons grapeseed
or sunflower oil

½ cup sliced shallots

1 teaspoon dried thyme

6 ounces button
mushrooms, sliced

7 ounces shiitake
mushrooms, sliced

3 garlic cloves, minced

1 teaspoon liquid smoke
(optional)

Growing up, I remember sitting with a huge bowl of green beans in my lap and snapping the ends off the beans while I watched TV and got my hair braided. We ate our green beans slow-cooked with smoked turkey necks. In this recipe, the beans are blanched to keep their nutrients, texture, and flavor.

1. Fill a stockpot with water and add 1 teaspoon of salt. Bring to a boil over medium-high heat.

2. Place the green beans in the boiling water and stir. Blanch for 3 to 4 minutes, until the beans are bright green but still firm.

3. While the beans are blanching, prepare a large bowl of ice water.

4. Remove the beans and immediately place in the ice water.

5. In a large nonstick sauté pan, heat the oil over medium-high heat. Once the oil is hot, add the shallots, thyme, button and shiitake mushrooms, and salt to taste, and stir. Cook for 6 to 8 minutes, allowing most of the liquid from the mushrooms to reabsorb, then add the garlic and liquid smoke (if using) and cook for another 1 to 2 minutes.

6. Drain the green beans and mix with the mushrooms in a large bowl. Serve hot.

Crispy Brussels Sprouts with Caramelized Onions and Cranberries

GLUTEN-FREE, NUT-FREE, SOY-FREE

SERVES 6 • PREP TIME: 15 MINUTES • COOK TIME: 30 MINUTES

1½ pounds Brussels sprouts

1 teaspoon crushed rosemary

¼ cup sunflower oil, plus 1 tablespoon sunflower oil or vegan butter, divided

Sea salt

Freshly ground black pepper

1 large yellow onion, chopped

¼ cup dried cranberries

I personally was not a fan of Brussels sprouts until I learned how to properly cook them in culinary school. I remember tasting the dish and then devouring the whole plate. That's how good they were. Brussels sprouts are anti-inflammatory and are high in fiber, protein, and vitamins A, C, and K, so no need to feel guilty if you actually want to eat a little more than a single portion of these.

1. Preheat the oven to 425°F. Line a baking pan with parchment paper.

2. Trim the bottom stems off the Brussels sprouts, then slice them in half and remove any discolored outer skins.

3. Place the Brussels sprouts in a medium bowl and sprinkle with the rosemary and ¼ cup of oil. Season with salt and pepper. Toss to ensure that all the Brussels sprouts are fully coated.

4. Pour the Brussels sprouts onto the lined baking pan, spreading to make a single layer, then bake for 25 to 30 minutes.

5. While the Brussels sprouts cook, in a medium cast-iron skillet or sauté pan over medium heat, heat the remaining 1 tablespoon of oil. Once the oil is

Continued

Crispy Brussels Sprouts with Caramelized Onions and Cranberries   *Continued*

hot, add the onion and a pinch of salt. Stir once, and then cook for 2 to 3 minutes without stirring to allow caramelization to begin. If the onions start to dry out, add a little water and stir.

6. Cook the onions for another 15 minutes, stirring occasionally. Remove from the heat when the onions have reached your desired color. The longer you cook them, the darker and more flavorful they will be. I typically make a large batch and cook them for about 25 minutes.

7. Once the Brussels sprouts have begun to crisp, remove them from the oven, place in a serving dish, sprinkle the onions and dried cranberries over the top, and serve.

....

Tip: For less crispy Brussels sprouts, bake only 15 to 20 minutes. Add chopped, toasted pecans or walnuts for additional crunch and texture.

Zesty Roasted Beets

GLUTEN-FREE, NUT-FREE, SOY-FREE

SERVES 6 • PREP TIME: 15 MINUTES • COOK TIME: 30 MINUTES

4 medium beets
1 tablespoon sunflower oil
½ teaspoon dried thyme
½ teaspoon crushed rosemary
Sea salt
Freshly ground black pepper
1 tablespoon white balsamic vinegar
1 tablespoon agave nectar

We all have that one vegetable that we could not stand as a child. For me, it was beets! While attending culinary school, I made orange-glazed beets in one of my classes and instantly fell in love! I'm pretty sure my mom was giving us canned beets, which I'm still not a fan of, but fresh beets roasted with herbs and love are absolutely delicious.

1. Preheat the oven to 400°F. Line a baking pan with parchment paper.

2. Wash and peel the beets and cut them into medium cubes. Place in a medium bowl, add the oil, thyme, and rosemary, and stir to combine. Season with salt and pepper.

3. Scatter the coated beets on the lined baking pan and bake for 25 to 30 minutes, or until fork-tender.

4. In a small bowl, whisk the vinegar and agave nectar.

5. Remove the cooked beets from the oven. Place in a serving dish and drizzle with the balsamic glaze to serve.

Tip: Beets are a tasty addition to any meal. I love to add them to leftover quinoa, rice, or salad greens for a nutritious, tasty, and quick meal.

Black-Eyed Pea Salad

GLUTEN-FREE, NUT-FREE, SOY-FREE, 30 MINUTES OR LESS

SERVES 6 • PREP TIME: 15 MINUTES

2 cups frozen black-eyed
    peas, thawed

1 cup frozen corn
    kernels, thawed

1 cucumber, seeded
    and diced

2 celery stalks, diced

1 orange or red bell pepper,
    seeded and diced

1 cup diced Roma
    tomatoes

½ cup chopped
    fresh parsley

½ cup chopped
    fresh cilantro

½ cup diced red onion

1 jalapeño, seeded and
    minced (optional)

1 tablespoon minced garlic

¼ cup sunflower oil

3 to 4 tablespoons
    lime juice

1 teaspoon sea salt

¼ teaspoon freshly ground
    black pepper

2 teaspoons agave nectar

Avocado slices, for topping

I love to eat this fresh, filling, and versatile salad with crackers, as a topping on green salad, or as a side dish with Caribbean Coconut Greens (page 62) and Buttermilk Biscuits (page 132) or Cornbread Waffles (page 131). Try it over cooked quinoa or rice for a quick and hearty meal.

1. In a large mixing bowl, combine the black-eyed peas, corn, cucumbers, celery, bell peppers, tomatoes, parsley, cilantro, onions, jalapeño (if using), and garlic. Stir and set aside.

2. In a small bowl, whisk together the oil, lime juice, salt, black pepper, and agave nectar until well combined.

3. Pour the dressing over the bean mixture, mix well, and serve topped with the avocado slices.

Tip: This salad can be served cold or at room temperature.

Fried Bananas

GLUTEN-FREE, NUT-FREE, 30 MINUTES OR LESS

SERVES 6 • PREP TIME: 5 MINUTES • COOK TIME: 5 TO 10 MINUTES

4 ripe bananas

2 tablespoons Earth
Balance vegan butter

4 tablespoons
agave nectar

1 teaspoon ground
cinnamon

Pinch sea salt

These fried bananas bring back fond memories whenever I make them. When I was growing up, my mother always had a plate of fried bananas or fried apples on the breakfast table on Sunday mornings when we ate pancakes or waffles. This recipe is easy, yummy, and definitely kid-approved.

1. Peel the bananas and cut them into 1½-inch-thick slices.

2. In a nonstick skillet over medium heat, combine the butter, agave nectar, cinnamon, and salt. As the butter begins to melt, stir together until a thin caramel forms.

3. Add the banana slices to the caramel sauce, cook for 2 to 3 minutes, and then turn to brown the other side. Be careful not to let the caramel get too dark or cook too fast, or the bananas will burn. Serve immediately.

Tip: Try to use bananas that are very ripe. The riper, the sweeter. Use as a topping on waffles, pancakes, or an open-face warm peanut butter–and-fried-banana sandwich. Store in a sealed container in the refrigerator for up to 3 days.

Pan-Fried Corn

GLUTEN-FREE, NUT-FREE, 30 MINUTES OR LESS

SERVES 6 TO 8 • PREP TIME: 10 MINUTES • COOK TIME: 15 MINUTES

4 tablespoons (½ stick)
vegan butter

1 red bell pepper, chopped

1 red onion, diced

3 garlic cloves, minced

½ teaspoon
smoked paprika

½ teaspoon onion powder

½ teaspoon thyme

Sea salt

Freshly ground
black pepper

3½ cups frozen
corn, thawed

This recipe is a remake of my mother's famous family dish. My mother could always get the most perfect caramelization on each kernel of corn with the globs of butter that her recipe called for. This recipe is my heart-healthy version.

1. Melt the butter in a large cast-iron pan or skillet over medium heat.

2. Add the bell peppers, onion, garlic, paprika, onion powder, and thyme and stir. Season with salt and pepper.

3. Cook for 2 to 3 minutes, then add the corn and stir.

4. Allow to cook for an additional 10 minutes, stirring frequently.

5. Once the corn starts to lightly brown, turn the heat off and serve.

Tip: Use any leftovers for chili and soups, or add to your cornbread waffles or hush puppies for extra texture and flavor.

Succotash

GLUTEN-FREE, NUT-FREE, 30 MINUTES OR LESS

SERVES 4 TO 6 • PREP TIME: 5 MINUTES • COOK TIME: 20 MINUTES

3 tablespoons Earth
    Balance vegan butter

1 red or orange bell
    pepper, diced

1 small red onion, diced

3 garlic cloves, minced

1 teaspoon dried thyme

1 teaspoon garlic powder

1 teaspoon onion powder

1 jalapeño, seeded
    and minced

3 ripe Roma
    tomatoes, chopped

Sea salt

Freshly ground
    black pepper

1½ cups frozen
    corn, thawed

1 cup frozen sliced
    okra, thawed

1 (10-ounce) package
    frozen lima
    beans, thawed

Succotash is a classic southern dish that serves as a side or as the main entrée when paired with rice or quinoa. The name "succotash" comes from the seventeenth-century Native American Narragansett language, in which "msickquatash" referred to a simmering pot of corn to which other ingredients were added. The dish can be enjoyed at any temperature.

1. Melt the butter in a large cast-iron pan or skillet. Add the bell peppers and onion and cook for 3 to 5 minutes, or just enough to soften.

2. Add the garlic, thyme, garlic powder, onion powder, jalapeño, and tomatoes and stir. Season with salt and pepper. Cook for another 2 minutes.

3. Add the corn, okra, and lima beans and stir. Cook for an additional 10 minutes, stirring frequently.

Herb-Roasted Root Vegetables

GLUTEN-FREE, NUT-FREE, SOY-FREE

SERVES 6 TO 8 • PREP TIME: 20 MINUTES • COOK TIME: 50 MINUTES

Nonstick cooking spray

1 large potato, cut into
1-inch cubes

1 large sweet potato,
peeled and cut into
1-inch cubes

2 small beets, peeled and
cut into 1-inch cubes

2 medium carrots,
halved and cut into
1½-inch cubes

1 parsnip, peeled and cut
into 1½-inch cubes

4 garlic cloves, minced

3 tablespoons
grapeseed oil

Sea salt

Freshly ground
black pepper

5 sprigs fresh thyme

5 sprigs fresh rosemary

One of the things I love about this recipe is the wonderful aroma of fresh herbs and vegetables roasting that fills my entire house. Every time I bake this dish, it takes me on a trip down memory lane and makes me think of family, holidays, and lots of love.

1. Preheat the oven to 425°F. Prepare a large baking pan with parchment paper or cooking spray.

2. In a large bowl, combine the potato, sweet potato, beets, carrots, parsnip, garlic, and oil, season with salt and pepper, and toss to coat well.

3. Place the vegetables on the baking pan in a single layer and top with the fresh thyme and rosemary sprigs.

4. Bake for 45 to 50 minutes. When the root vegetables are lightly browned and fork-tender, they are done.

Country Vegetable
Pot Pie, *page 102*

Chapter Six
Mains

Lentil and Sweet Potato Shepherd's Pie

GLUTEN-FREE, NUT-FREE

SERVES 6 TO 8 • PREP TIME: 15 MINUTES • COOK TIME: 1 HOUR 10 MINUTES

FOR THE TOPPING

Nonstick cooking spray
2 pounds sweet potatoes
2 tablespoons Earth
    Balance vegan butter
¼ teaspoon freshly ground
    black pepper
½ cup coconut milk

FOR THE FILLING

1 cup dried lentils
2 teaspoons dried thyme
2 bay leaves
3 cups water
½ teaspoon sea salt
1 tablespoon sunflower oil
2 cups chopped baby
    portobello mushrooms
1 teaspoon onion powder
1 cup diced celery
½ cup chopped carrot
1 teaspoon parsley
1 cup diced red onion
1 teaspoon rosemary
3 garlic cloves, minced
½ cup vegetable stock

Shepherd's pie is not necessarily a southern dish, but this and several other comfort food classics can easily cross over into soul food territory by swapping in ingredients like sweet potatoes for white potatoes.

1. Preheat the oven to 425°F. Prepare a baking pan with parchment paper or cooking spray.

2. Wash and dry the sweet potatoes. Place them on the baking pan and use a fork to prick holes all over.

3. Bake for 30 to 40 minutes, until fork-tender through the middle.

4. Meanwhile, make the filling. In a medium saucepan, combine the lentils, thyme, bay leaves, water, and salt. Bring to a boil, then cover and reduce the heat to simmer for 25 to 30 minutes. Remove the bay leaves from the cooked lentils.

5. Remove the potatoes from the oven and allow to cool about 10 minutes. Remove the skins and place the flesh in a large mixing bowl with the butter, black pepper, and coconut milk. Blend with a handheld mixer on medium speed for 2 to 3 minutes or until well mixed and fluffy, then set aside.

6. Heat the oil in a large skillet over medium heat, then add the mushrooms, onion powder, celery, carrots, parsley, onion, rosemary, and garlic and stir. Cook until the onions become translucent, then add

the lentils and vegetable stock and cook another 15 minutes, or until the lentils have softened but still have some firmness.

7. Transfer the hot lentil mixture into a coated 9-by-9-inch baking dish, spread evenly with a spatula, top with the sweet potato mixture, and spread evenly.

8. Bake for 15 minutes or until the potato top has slightly browned.

9. Remove from the oven, cool for 5 to 10 minutes, and serve.

Cajun Fried "Chicken"

NUT-FREE, 30 MINUTES OR LESS

SERVES 4 • PREP TIME: 15 MINUTES • COOK TIME: 15 MINUTES

FOR THE DRY MIX

1½ cups gluten-free flour

1 tablespoon Creole Cajun Seasoning (page 123)

1 teaspoon granulated garlic

Sea salt

FOR THE WET MIX

½ cup Frank's RedHot sauce

1½ cups unbleached all-purpose flour

½ cup plant-based milk

FOR THE "CHICKEN"

Nonstick cooking spray

1½ cups grapeseed oil, for frying

4 small clusters oyster mushrooms

Fried chicken ranks up near the top for soul food cuisine. My version uses the meaty oyster mushroom, seasoned and fried to perfection and guaranteed to satisfy that fried-chicken craving. Oyster mushrooms can usually be found at your local international or Asian market.

1. In a medium mixing bowl, whisk the dry mix ingredients to combine.

2. In another medium mixing bowl, whisk the wet mix ingredients to combine.

3. Prepare a baking pan with parchment paper or cooking spray and set aside.

4. In a saucepan, heat the oil over medium-high heat. Line up the wet mix, the dry mix, and the baking pan.

5. Add the mushrooms one at a time to the wet mix, lightly shake off any excess, roll in the dry mix, and then set on the baking pan. Continue until all the mushrooms are dredged.

6. Gently place the coated mushrooms into the hot oil and fry until golden brown, 3 to 4 minutes on each side.

7. Remove from the oil, drain on a paper bag, and serve with your favorite southern sides.

Tip: Fried mushrooms are best eaten immediately. To reheat, the best method is to use an air fryer.

Peach-Habanero Barbecue Lentil Mini Loaves

NUT-FREE, SOY-FREE

SERVES 6 • PREP TIME: 15 MINUTES • COOK TIME: 1 HOUR

1 cup dried lentils

2½ cups water

1 teaspoon dried thyme

3 tablespoons flax meal

⅓ cup warm water

2 tablespoons sunflower oil

½ cup diced onion

1½ teaspoons granulated garlic

1 celery stalk, diced

½ cup small diced carrots

1 cup diced green or red bell pepper

1 teaspoon cumin

1 teaspoon smoked paprika

1 teaspoon onion powder

1 teaspoon chili powder

1 teaspoon liquid smoke

Sea salt

Freshly ground black pepper

¾ cup oats

½ cup unbleached all-purpose flour

Nonstick cooking spray

½ cup Peach-Habanero Barbecue Sauce (page 117)

These mini loaves are a perfect and flavorful replacement for the traditional ground meat version. Lentils are inexpensive, hearty, and nutrient dense. This recipe makes perfect individual loaves, which can be served as an entrée for any holiday meal or get-together.

1. Preheat the oven to 375°F.

2. Rinse the lentils and place in a medium pot with the water and thyme. Bring to a boil, cover, and reduce the heat to simmer for 30 minutes, or until the lentils are soft and the liquid is absorbed.

3. In a small bowl, combine the flax meal and warm water, stir, and allow to thicken.

4. In a medium saucepan over medium heat, heat the oil, then add the onion, granulated garlic, celery, carrots, bell peppers, cumin, smoked paprika, onion powder, chili powder, and liquid smoke, and season with salt and black pepper. Stir and cook until the onions are translucent and the seasonings are very fragrant. Remove from the heat and set aside.

5. Remove the bay leaf from the cooked lentils. Place the cooked lentils in a large mixing bowl and add the veggie mixture, flax mixture, oats, and flour and mix until well combined.

Continued

Peach-Habanero Barbecue Lentil Mini Loaves *Continued*

6. Coat a mini loaf pan with cooking spray, then fill each loaf well with the lentil mixture. Use the palm of your hand to make a little hump on the top of each loaf.

7. Using a pastry brush, brush the tops of the loaves with the barbecue sauce.

8. Bake for 15 to 18 minutes or until the loaves become firm and the barbecue sauce develops a nice, dark glaze.

9. Allow to cool for 10 minutes, then gently remove from the pan and serve.

....

Tip: Serve with Garlic-Smashed Potatoes (page 71) and Crispy Brussels Sprouts with Caramelized Onions and Cranberries (page 77).

Acorn Squash Stuffed with Cornbread Stuffing

NUT-FREE, SOY-FREE

SERVES 6 • PREP TIME: 15 MINUTES • COOK TIME: 35 MINUTES

3 acorn squash, washed
  and halved
Nonstick cooking spray
2 tablespoons
  grapeseed oil
1 cup diced onion
1 medium carrot, diced
2 celery stalks, diced
2 garlic cloves, minced
⅓ cup dried cranberries
2 tablespoons rubbed sage
2 teaspoons thyme
½ cup vegetable stock
Sea salt
Freshly ground
  black pepper
4 cups Skillet Cornbread,
  cubed (page 138)
⅓ cup pumpkin seeds

Acorn squash is considered a winter squash and is tasty in savory or sweet dishes. This recipe can be made for any occasion, but I love to serve this as a main option for Thanksgiving or Christmas. Stuffing the squash with cornbread gives this dish a true southern flair.

1. Preheat the oven to 400°F.

2. Scoop out the seeds and membranes from each squash half, then use cooking spray to coat the inside and outside of each half. Place facedown on a baking pan lined with parchment paper or coated with more cooking spray. Bake for 20 minutes, or until the center is fork-tender.

3. Heat the oil in a saucepan over medium heat, then add the onion, carrots, celery, garlic, cranberries, sage, thyme, and vegtable stock. Season with salt and pepper. Stir to combine and cook for 5 minutes or until the onions are translucent.

4. In a large bowl, combine the cornbread cubes, the pumpkin seeds, and the vegetable mixture.

5. Once the squash has cooled, fill each half with stuffing and bake for an additional 10 minutes, or until the stuffing is firm and browned on top.

6. Remove from the oven and let cool for 5 minutes.

Tip: This squash can be stuffed with rice and veggies and topped with vegan cheese as a replacement for the cornbread.

Buffalo Popcorn Chickenless Bites

GLUTEN-FREE, NUT-FREE, 30 MINUTES OR LESS

SERVES 6 • PREP TIME: 20 MINUTES • COOK TIME: 5 MINUTES

2 (14-ounce) packages extra-firm tofu, frozen and thawed

1½ cups grapeseed oil

½ cup cornstarch

1 cup Frank's RedHot sauce

⅓ cup sunflower oil

⅓ cup maple syrup

Celery or carrot sticks, for serving

Freezing tofu gives it a meatier texture and actually makes it my favorite chicken replacement. I only buy organic, non-GMO tofu, as soybeans are in the top three foods that are genetically modified and among the highest in pesticides.

1. To press the tofu, place it in a strainer, put a paper towel over the top, and set a plate with two cans on top to push the water out. Allow to drain for at least 20 minutes.

2. In a medium pot, heat the grapeseed oil to 375°F for frying.

3. Put the cornstarch in a medium mixing bowl. In another bowl, whisk together the hot sauce, sunflower oil, and maple syrup to make the buffalo sauce.

4. Tear the drained tofu into bite-size pieces and toss in the cornstarch until fully coated.

5. Gently drop the coated bites into the hot oil and fry for 2 minutes or until lightly golden brown and firmly crisp.

6. Remove the bites from the oil, toss in the buffalo sauce, and serve with celery or carrots sticks.

Tip: These are great with any kind of barbecue sauce, or whip up a quick agave-mustard sauce by mixing 3 tablespoons of your favorite mustard with 2 tablespoons of agave nectar, 1 teaspoon of rice vinegar, and 2 tablespoons of vegan mayo.

Fried Okra

NUT-FREE

SERVES 6 • PREP TIME: 15 MINUTES • COOK TIME: 25 MINUTES

3 to 4 cups sunflower oil
for frying or coconut oil
spray for baking

1 cup unbleached
all-purpose
flour, divided

½ cup unsweetened
plant-based milk

⅓ cup cornmeal

1 teaspoon
granulated garlic

1 teaspoon Creole Cajun
Seasoning (page 123)

Sea salt

Freshly ground
black pepper

1½ pounds okra

Okra is one of those vegetables that is not really a vegetable but actually a fruit. Most people either like or dislike okra; there is usually no in-between. I grew up eating handfuls of crispy fried okra as a snack, so I love it. Studies have shown that okra is beneficial for stabilizing blood sugar for diabetics. This recipe can be prepared fried or baked. I love it with Hush Puppies (page 67) and Fried Cabbage (page 74).

1. If baking, preheat the oven to 425°F and prepare a baking pan with parchment paper or coconut oil spray. If frying, heat the sunflower oil in a medium saucepan over medium heat.

2. In a small bowl, whisk ½ cup of flour and the milk to combine. In another small bowl, put the cornmeal, the remaining ½ cup of flour, the granulated garlic, and the Cajun seasoning, season with salt and pepper, and stir to mix well.

3. A few pieces at a time, add the okra to the wet mix, shake off any extra wet mix, and then toss in the dry mix. Once the okra are fully coated, if baking, place them on the baking pan and bake for 20 to 25 minutes, or until crisp and golden brown. If frying, add several pieces of okra to the hot oil and cook for 3 to 4 minutes, making sure to turn. Once the okra are golden brown on all sides, remove from the oil and drain on paper bags or towels. Serve immediately.

Salisbury Lentil Steaks

NUT-FREE

SERVES 6 • PREP TIME: 15 MINUTES • COOK TIME: 25 MINUTES

FOR THE STEAKS

3 tablespoons flax meal

1 cup warm water, divided

½ cup textured vegetable protein (TVP)

2 cups canned lentils, rinsed

½ teaspoon granulated garlic

½ teaspoon onion powder

½ teaspoon dried oregano

1 teaspoon salt

Freshly ground black pepper

2 teaspoons vegan Worcestershire sauce

⅓ cup bread crumbs, or more if needed

⅓ cup flour

1 tablespoon sunflower oil

FOR THE GRAVY

4 tablespoons sunflower oil

½ cup sliced white button mushrooms

1 medium onion, thinly sliced

½ teaspoon dried thyme

1 teaspoon sea salt

Freshly ground black pepper

4 teaspoons flour

Salisbury steak with onions and gravy is a southern favorite. Think of hamburgers smothered in a creamy, flavorful onion gravy. Of course, this recipe omits the burger, but it has two wonderfully protein-packed, delicious meat replacements instead: textured vegetable protein (TVP) and lentils. Your taste buds are going to love this dish.

To make the steaks

1. In a small bowl, mix the flax with ⅓ cup of warm water, stir, and set aside for 5 minutes. In a separate small bowl, cover the TVP with ½ cup of warm water and soak for 5 minutes to rehydrate.

2. In a food processor, put the lentils, rehydrated TVP, flax mixture, granulated garlic, onion powder, oregano, salt, pepper, and Worcestershire sauce and pulse together until well combined. Remove the lid, and add the bread crumbs, flour, and a little water. Pulse again until well combined.

3. When the mixture is ready, it will be firm enough to form a ball. Form "steak" patties and set aside.

4. In a large saucepan, heat the oil. Add the patties and cook until browned on each side.

4 cups vegetable stock or unsweetened plant-based milk

To make the gravy

1. In the same pan, combine the oil, mushrooms, onion, and thyme, season with salt and pepper, and cook for 4 to 5 minutes or until the onions are soft.

2. Stir in the flour, turn the heat down, and allow the roux to get a rich brown. Do not allow it to get too dark or to burn. Slowly add in the veggie stock while stirring with a whisk to prevent clumping.

3. Once the gravy starts to thicken, add the patties and allow them to cook in the gravy for 10 to 15 minutes. Serve.

Fishless Banana-Blossom Fish

NUT-FREE, SOY-FREE

SERVES 4 • PREP TIME: 15 MINUTES, PLUS 1 HOUR TO MARINATE • COOK TIME: 15 MINUTES

FOR THE "FISH"

1 (20-ounce) can of Aroy-D
    banana blossoms,
    in brine

FOR THE MARINADE

2 cups water

1 teaspoon kelp powder

1 nori sheet, crumbled

Oil for frying

FOR THE DRY MIX

1 cup unbleached
    all-purpose flour

1 teaspoon salt, or more
    to taste

Freshly ground
    black pepper

½ teaspoon
    granulated garlic

½ teaspoon dried parsley

FOR THE WET MIX

1 cup unbleached
    all-purpose flour

½ cup sparkling water

½ teaspoon Old Bay
    seasoning

2 teaspoons lemon juice

Fish was one of the hardest things to give up when I went vegan. I loved seafood and could eat it every day. While living in the Virgin Islands, I was exposed to many different fruits and vegetables that could be used as meat replacements. Banana blossoms are the flowers from the banana tree. They can be eaten raw or cooked. You'll be amazed at how this flower has the same texture as cod and, when seasoned, actually really tastes like fish!

1. Strain and rinse the banana blossoms. In a medium glass bowl with a lid, create a marinade by combining the water, kelp powder, and nori crumbles. Gently place the banana blossoms in the marinade and allow to sit for at least 1 hour in the refrigerator.

2. In a medium bowl, mix the dry ingredients. In a shallow pan, mix the wet ingredients.

3. In a medium saucepot, heat the oil for frying over medium heat.

4. Gently place the banana blossoms one at a time in the wet mix and then the dry mix, and then place in the hot oil. Cook for 4 to 5 minutes or until golden brown, then turn and cook on the other side.

5. Remove the blossoms from the oil, drain on a paper bag, and serve.

Tip: Serve with Avocado Slaw (page 34) and Tartar Sauce (page 121).

Jerk Barbecue-Pulled Mushrooms

GLUTEN-FREE, NUT-FREE, SOY-FREE

SERVES 6 • PREP TIME: 15 MINUTES • COOK TIME: 20 MINUTES

8 king oyster mushrooms
½ teaspoon Creole Cajun Seasoning (page 123)
1 tablespoon minced garlic
1½ teaspoons smoked paprika
½ teaspoon liquid smoke
Pinch salt
3 tablespoons sunflower oil
Nonstick cooking spray
¾ cup Jerk Barbecue Sauce (page 119)

These mushrooms are delicious and surprisingly easy to make. Oyster mushrooms are low in calories and high in protein and fiber, so they make a nutritious meat replacement. These are great in a sandwich or on top of a cornbread waffle. Serve with Avocado Slaw (page 34) and top with crispy onions (from the Heirlooom Tomato and Avocado Stacks recipe, page 31) for a flavorful and delicious meal.

1. Preheat the oven to 400°F.

2. Place the mushrooms on a plate and use two forks to pull them apart, starting at the bottom and using the full mushroom, including the cap and stem. Continue until all the mushrooms are shredded.

3. Sprinkle the mushrooms with the Cajun seasoning, garlic, paprika, liquid smoke, salt, and oil and mix with your hands.

4. On a baking pan lined with parchment paper or sprayed with cooking spray, spread out the seasoned mushrooms evenly.

5. Bake for 15 minutes.

6. Remove the pan from the oven, drizzle the barbecue sauce over the mushrooms, and mix well.

7. Bake for another 5 minutes, allowing the barbecue sauce to glaze the mushrooms.

8. Remove from the oven and serve.

Country-Fried Mushroom Steaks

NUT-FREE, OIL-FREE, SOY-FREE, 30 MINUTES OR LESS

SERVES 4 • PREP TIME: 15 MINUTES • COOK TIME: 15 MINUTES

Nonstick cooking spray

1½ cups aquafaba

½ cup unbleached
    all-purpose flour

5 tablespoons cornmeal

½ teaspoon dried sage

½ teaspoon dried thyme

½ teaspoon
    granulated garlic

½ teaspoon onion powder

½ teaspoon dried parsley

½ teaspoon
    smoked paprika

Sea salt

Freshly ground
    black pepper

4 large portobello
    mushrooms, cleaned
    and stemmed

Portobello mushrooms have a meaty texture and flavor, perfect for this dish. In this recipe I use aquafaba, which is the brine or juice from chickpeas. This magical liquid can be used as an egg white replacement in vegan cooking and baking. In this recipe, the aquafaba is lightly whipped for use as a wet coating for the mushroom steaks.

1. Preheat the oven to 400°F. Line a baking pan with parchment paper or spray with cooking spray.

2. In a medium mixing bowl, whip the aquafaba using a hand mixer on low for 1 to 2 minutes, just until the aquafaba is slightly fluffy, then set aside.

3. In a shallow pan, combine the flour, cornmeal, sage, thyme, granulated garlic, onion powder, parsley, and paprika, season with salt and pepper, and mix well.

4. Dip the portobello caps one at a time into the aquafaba, then roll in the flour mixture on both sides and place on the prepared baking pan.

5. Bake the mushroom steaks for 12 to 15 minutes, or until browned and crispy. A fork should easily pierce the middle when done.

6. Let cool for 2 to 3 minutes, then serve.

Tip: If you prefer a richer taste, you can fry these dredged mushrooms in a saucepan over medium heat using ⅓ cup of oil, cooking for 5 to 6 minutes on each side.

Country-Style Fried Green Tomatoes

GLUTEN-FREE, NUT-FREE, 30 MINUTES OR LESS

SERVES 6 • PREP TIME: 15 MINUTES • COOK TIME: 15 MINUTES

3 green tomatoes

⅓ cup cornmeal

½ teaspoon Creole Cajun Seasoning (page 123)

Sea salt

Freshly ground black pepper

¼ cup unsweetened plant-based milk

¼ cup aquafaba

Oil for frying

This southern staple is such a treat. Green tomatoes are just unripe tomatoes, and they do not need to be a special variety. These babies are delicious made into sandwiches like a BLAT (tempeh bacon, lettuce, avocado, and tomato) or served as a main dish along with greens and Hush Puppies (page 67).

1. Wash the tomatoes, and then slice each into 4 to 5 slices about ½ inch thick.

2. In a shallow dish, combine the cornmeal, Cajun seasoning, salt, and pepper.

3. In another shallow dish, combine the milk and aquafaba and whisk to blend well.

4. In a skillet, heat a generous amount of oil for frying.

5. Coat the tomato slices by first dipping into the milk mixture and then tossing in the flour mixture, making sure both sides are fully dredged.

6. Gently place each slice in the hot oil and fry for 3 to 4 minutes on each side, until golden brown.

7. Once both sides are cooked, remove from the oil, drain on a paper bag, and serve immediately.

Country Vegetable Pot Pie

NUT-FREE, SOY-FREE

SERVES 6 • PREP TIME: 15 MINUTES • COOK TIME: 35 MINUTES

2 tablespoons sunflower oil

1 medium onion, diced

2 celery stalks, chopped

1 medium carrot, chopped

1 cup sliced baby
    portobello mushrooms

1 medium sweet potato,
    peeled and diced

1 teaspoon
    granulated garlic

2 garlic cloves, minced

1 teaspoon dried thyme

1 teaspoon smoked paprika

1 teaspoon crushed
    rosemary

2 cups stemmed and
    roughly chopped kale

1 cup stemmed and
    roughly chopped
    Swiss chard

2 tablespoons unbleached
    all-purpose flour

2 cups vegetable stock

Sea salt

Freshly ground
    black pepper

1 (16-ounce) package
    phyllo dough

This veggie-packed savory pie is perfect for an easy, comforting dinner. I typically use whatever vegetables I already have in my refrigerator. I suggest trying this recipe a time or two and then playing around with different ingredients that you may have on hand to make it your own.

1. Preheat the oven to 375°F.

2. In a medium stockpot, heat the oil over medium heat. Once the oil is hot, add the onion, celery, carrots, mushrooms, sweet potatoes, granulated garlic, minced garlic, thyme, smoked paprika, and rosemary and stir. Allow to cook for about 10 minutes, or until the sweet potatoes are slightly tender and the seasonings become very fragrant.

3. Add the kale and chard and cook for another 2 minutes, stirring frequently. Add the flour and stir until well combined. Slowly add the stock and salt and pepper to taste. Allow to thicken, and then transfer the mixture to an oiled medium baking dish.

4. Unroll the phyllo dough and gently place on top of the veggie mixture. Use a knife to make three slits in the middle of the dough, and then bake for 20 minutes, or until the top is golden brown and the filling is bubbling around the sides.

5. Remove from the oven and allow to cool for 5 to 10 minutes before serving.

Jambalaya

NUT-FREE, SOY-FREE

SERVES 6 TO 8 • PREP TIME: 15 MINUTES • COOK TIME: 50 MINUTES

2½ tablespoons sunflower oil, divided

1 large onion, diced

2 celery stalks, chopped

1 medium carrot, chopped

2 red bell peppers, diced

2 cups sliced baby portobello mushrooms

1 teaspoon Creole Cajun Seasoning (page 123)

1 habanero pepper

2½ teaspoons Blackened Seasoning (page 122)

1 (15-ounce) can fire-roasted diced tomatoes

1 tablespoon tomato paste

Sea salt

Freshly ground black pepper

2 cups long-grain brown rice, uncooked

Hot sauce

4 bay leaves

4 cups vegetable stock

1 package Field Roast spicy or apple-sage sausage, sliced

1½ cups cooked kidney beans

¼ cup chopped fresh parsley (optional, for garnish)

Jambalaya originated in New Orleans around the eighteenth century. Traditionally, this dish is made with pork, andouille sausage, and seafood with spices and rice all cooked in a broth. I recreated this flavorful dish using veggies and vegan sausage along with the traditional creole seasonings and rice to keep the authentic taste and heartiness of the classic version.

1. In a medium stockpot, heat 2 tablespoons of oil over medium heat. Add the onion, celery, carrots, bell peppers, and mushrooms and stir. Cook until the onions have softened, 3 to 5 minutes. Add the Cajun seasoning, habanero pepper, Blackened Seasoning, diced tomatoes, and tomato paste, season with salt and pepper, stir, and cook for another 3 to 4 minutes.

2. Stir in the rice, hot sauce, bay leaves, and stock, then turn the heat up and bring to a boil. Cover, reduce the heat, and allow to cook covered for 30 minutes or until all the liquid has evaporated.

3. While the rice is cooking, heat the remaining ½ tablespoon of oil in a saucepan over medium-high heat, then add the sausage to brown on both sides. Mix in the kidney beans.

4. Once the rice is cooked, remove the pot from the heat, and allow to sit covered for another 10 minutes.

5. Remove the bay leaves and fluff the rice with a fork, then add in the sausage and beans, and stir to combine.

6. Top with the parsley if desired and serve.

Blackened Cauliflower Steaks

GLUTEN-FREE, NUT-FREE, SOY-FREE

SERVES 4 • PREP TIME: 10 MINUTES • COOK TIME: 30 MINUTES

1 large head cauliflower

Nonstick cooking spray

1 tablespoon grapeseed or sunflower oil

½ teaspoon liquid smoke

2 tablespoons Blackened Seasoning (page 122)

I've created several cauliflower dishes over the years, but these steaks are so easy, flavorful, and filling that I love making them the most. By using different seasoning blends, like Indian curry or Moroccan spices, these steaks can become the main dish for any type of cuisine. Blackening is a traditional southern technique in which the meat is typically brushed with butter and then coated with blackening seasoning and pan-fried. This recipe uses oil in place of butter and is baked to make it even healthier.

1. Preheat the oven to 400°F.

2. Clean the cauliflower and trim the green leaves off the bottom. Slice the sides off the cauliflower to allow for even steaks, then cut into 4 (½-inch-thick) steaks and place them on a baking pan lined with parchment paper or coated with cooking spray.

3. In a small bowl, mix the oil and the liquid smoke.

4. Brush the oil mixture onto both sides of each steak, then rub the Blackened Seasoning onto each side.

5. Roast the cauliflower steaks for 15 minutes on each side or until the edges of each steak have slightly blackened and the middle is firm but fork-tender.

6. Remove from the oven, use a large spatula to gently place each steak on a plate, and serve with your favorite sides.

Creole Fried Rice

GLUTEN-FREE, NUT-FREE, SOY-FREE

SERVES 6 • PREP TIME: 30 MINUTES, PLUS OVERNIGHT FOR THE RICE • COOK TIME: 25 MINUTES

1 cup brown basmati rice

1½ cups water

1 tablespoon sunflower oil

1 large onion, diced

2 celery stalks, chopped

1 medium carrot, chopped

1 yellow bell pepper, diced

½ cup baby portobello
    mushrooms

3 garlic cloves, minced

2 cups frozen okra

1½ cups corn

1 cup frozen black-eyed
    peas, thawed

1 cup canned kidney
    beans, rinsed
    and drained

2 or 3 dashes hot sauce

1 teaspoon
    smoked paprika

1 teaspoon thyme

1 teaspoon oregano

1 teaspoon Creole Cajun
    Seasoning (page 123)

Sea salt

Freshly ground
    black pepper

This dish is cooked just like the more well-known Chinese dish, but with southern flavors. It is a fun way to fuse cuisines for a really unique entrée. It tastes best using day-old rice, so cook the rice a day ahead and store refrigerated in a sealed container if you don't already have leftovers. It is also a great way to use up leftover veggies.

1. The day before, cook the rice with the water in a rice cooker or saucepot. Once the rice is cooked, fluff with a fork, transfer to a bowl set in an ice bath to cool, and then cover and place in the refrigerator overnight.

2. In a large skillet, heat the oil over medium heat, then add the onion, celery, carrots, bell peppers, mushrooms, and garlic and stir. Cook until the onions are softened.

3. Add the okra, corn, black-eyed peas, beans, hot sauce, smoked paprika, thyme, oregano, and Cajun seasoning, season with salt and black pepper, and cook for 10 to 15 minutes longer.

4. Add the rice to the skillet with the okra and corn mixture and stir to combine well.

5. Continue cooking for 3 to 5 minutes or until the rice is thoroughly heated, then serve.

Crispy Cauliflower Wings

NUT-FREE, OIL-FREE, 30 MINUTES OR LESS

SERVES 4 TO 6 • PREP TIME: 15 MINUTES • COOK TIME: 15 MINUTES

¾ cup unbleached
    all-purpose flour
1 cup unsweetened
    plant-based milk
½ teaspoon
    smoked paprika
1 teaspoon
    granulated garlic
½ teaspoon onion powder
½ teaspoon sea salt
2 pinches freshly ground
    black pepper
2½ cups panko
    bread crumbs
1 large head cauliflower,
    cut into bite-size florets

These wings are one of our biggest sellers at my restaurant. They are crispy, crunchy, and packed with flavor to satisfy that wing craving. Plus, they are easy to make! Serve these wings with sliced cucumber, carrots, and celery on the side, along with jerk barbecue or buffalo sauce for dipping.

1. Preheat the oven to 400°F. Line a baking pan with parchment paper.

2. In a shallow dish, combine the flour, milk, paprika, granulated garlic, onion powder, salt, and black pepper and whisk until well combined.

3. Pour the panko bread crumbs into a separate shallow dish.

4. Dip 1 floret at a time into the wet mix, then toss in the panko bread crumbs, turning until fully coated. Place each battered floret on the baking pan, continuing until all the florets are battered.

5. Bake until golden brown and crispy, 12 to 15 minutes.

6. Remove from the oven, plate, and serve.

Barbecue Riblets

NUT-FREE, OIL-FREE

SERVES 6 TO 8 • PREP TIME: 15 MINUTES • COOK TIME: 1 HOUR 5 MINUTES

1 tablespoon
    smoked paprika

3 tablespoons
    nutritional yeast

2 teaspoons onion powder

2 teaspoons
    granulated garlic

2 tablespoons tamari or
    soy sauce

1 teaspoon liquid smoke

¾ cup water

1½ cups vital wheat gluten

1 (20-ounce) can green
    jackfruit in brine,
    strained and rinsed

1 cup Jerk Barbecue Sauce
    (page 119)

Meat-eaters love this finger-licking dish, while some vegans miss the classic flavors and textures they grew up on. The traditional recipe slow-cooks or smokes meat for hours to give it tenderness and smoky flavor. My recipe uses wheat gluten and jackfruit to give these mock ribs a meaty texture that is sure to please. Serve with Candied Yams (page 70), Cornbread Waffles (page 131), and Caribbean Coconut Greens (page 62).

1. Preheat the oven to 375°F.

2. In a food processor, combine the paprika, nutritional yeast, onion powder, granulated garlic, tamari, liquid smoke, and water and pulse until well blended. Add the vital wheat gluten and blend until well combined.

3. In a medium bowl, use a masher to mash the jackfruit until it begins to break down. Add the jackfruit to the gluten mixture in the food processor and pulse 3 to 5 times or until the jackfruit is well incorporated.

4. Remove the mixture from the food processor and divide into four equal balls. Partially flatten out each ball, forming a rectangle about ¾ inch thick. With a sharp knife, make deep slices into the dough to create the look of ribs.

5. Cut four pieces of parchment and four pieces of aluminum foil, each 10 to 12 inches square. Place the parchment inside the foil to create a packet, add a riblet, and then fold the edges to seal the packet and place on a baking pan. Repeat for each riblet.

Continued

Barbecue Riblets *Continued*

6. In a stockpot fitted with a steam insert, place the four slabs, taking care to avoid overlapping them as much as possible. Steam for 30 minutes.

7. After the slabs are steamed, place on a baking pan and bake for 20 to 25 minutes.

8. Open the packets and brush each riblet with barbecue sauce, then cook with the packet open for another 5 to 10 minutes or until the riblets are firm.

9. Take out of the oven and serve.

Jalapeño Hoe Cakes

NUT-FREE, 30 MINUTES OR LESS

SERVES 6 TO 8 • PREP TIME: 15 MINUTES • COOK TIME: 15 MINUTES

1 cup unbleached
all-purpose flour

1 cup yellow corn meal

1½ cups frozen corn

1 cup unsweetened
plant-based milk

1 tablespoon agave nectar

1 teaspoon baking powder

1 teaspoon sea salt

⅔ cup unsweetened
applesauce

1 jalapeño, diced

1 teaspoon
granulated garlic

1 teaspoon onion powder

Pinch smoked paprika

3 tablespoons melted
vegan butter or oil

Hoe cakes are corn cakes that are fun, easy, and delicious. With little prep and a quick cooking time, this dish can be made as a quick dinner or a tasty side. Serve with Jerk Barbecue-Pulled Mushrooms (page 99) or your favorite stews.

1. In a medium bowl, combine all the ingredients except the butter and whisk until well combined.

2. Heat the butter in a cast-iron pan or skillet over medium heat.

3. Use an ice cream scoop to scoop the batter in portions into the hot pan. Cook until the cakes are golden brown and air bubbles start to form. Then turn and cook on the other side.

4. Once both sides are fully cooked, remove the cakes from the pan, drain on a paper bag, and serve.

Tip: Using a cast-iron pan enhances the flavor of any dish, and with these cakes it creates extra crispiness.

Crispy Fishless Po'boy Sliders

NUT-FREE, SOY-FREE, 30 MINUTES OR LESS

SERVES 6 • PREP TIME: 10 MINUTES, IF USING PREVIOUSLY PREPARED "FISH" •
COOK TIME: 20 MINUTES

6 Fishless Banana-Blossom Fish (page 98)
1 fresh baguette, cut into 6 pieces
1½ teaspoon Creole Cajun seasoning (page 123)
½ cup vegan mayo
6 romaine lettuce leaves
1 beefsteak tomato, sliced
12 dill pickles, thickly sliced

To recreate this southern dish, banana blossoms are the perfect choice. These flowers give this sandwich exactly the taste and texture to fool any fish lover. When I was growing up, sandwiches were usually only made with wheat bread, and that's usually how we made our fish sandwiches. I remember having my first po'boy in my teens. What stuck out was the crispness of the bread and the sauce that made the sandwich oh-so-amazing.

1. Preheat the oven to 375°F.

2. Place the prepared banana-blossom "fish" on a baking pan in the oven to warm. Slice the baguette pieces in half horizontally and warm in the oven for 3 to 4 minutes.

3. While the bread is warming, in a small bowl, combine the Cajun seasoning and the vegan mayo and whisk to mix well, creating a Creole aioli.

4. Take the bread and banana blossoms out of the oven and place the bread on plates. Spread the Creole aioli on both sides of the bread, then add the lettuce, tomato slices, pickles, and banana-blossom "fish" and serve immediately.

Mushroom and Sweet Potato Burgers

GLUTEN-FREE, NUT-FREE, SOY-FREE

SERVES 6 TO 8 • PREP TIME: 15 MINUTES • COOK TIME: 45 MINUTES

Nonstick cooking spray
½ cup quinoa
1 cup water
1 large sweet potato
1 tablespoon flax meal
3 tablespoons warm water
1 teaspoon grapeseed oil
**8 ounces baby portobello
  mushrooms, chopped**
⅓ red onion, chopped
**½ cup frozen kidney
  beans, thawed**
**½ cup red bell
  pepper, chopped**
1½ teaspoons cumin
**1 teaspoon
  granulated garlic**
½ teaspoon onion powder
**1 teaspoon
  smoked paprika**
**½ teaspoon adobo sauce
  from canned chipotles**

This burger is filled with protein and packs a flavor punch. If you want to impress your meat-eating friends, this burger is just the dish. Serve on your favorite bun topped with sliced avocado, Jerk Barbecue Sauce (page 119), and crispy onions. Fresh-made biscuits are my favorite bun for these burgers. Add a side of Zucchini and Eggplant Fries (page 72), Fried Cabbage (page 74), or Avocado Slaw (page 34) for a complete meal.

1. Preheat the oven to 400°F. Line a baking pan with parchment paper or spray with cooking spray.

2. In a medium pot, combine the quinoa and 1 cup of water and bring to a boil over medium heat. Reduce the heat to low, cover, and allow to simmer for 20 minutes.

3. While the quinoa cooks, peel the sweet potato and cut it into 1-inch cubes.

4. Place the sweet potato cubes on the prepared baking pan and bake for 10 to 15 minutes, or until fork-tender.

5. Meanwhile, mix the flax meal and 3 tablespoons of warm water in a small bowl and let sit for 5 to 10 minutes.

Continued

Mushroom and Sweet Potato Burgers *Continued*

6. In a skillet, heat the oil over medium-high heat. Once the oil is hot, add the mushrooms, onion, beans, bell peppers, cumin, granulated garlic, onion powder, smoked paprika, and adobo sauce. Cook for 5 minutes, or until the onions are translucent, then remove from the heat.

7. Combine ½ cup of the cooked quinoa, the sweet potato cubes, the mushroom mixture, and the flax mixture in a food processor and pulse until well blended.

8. Remove the mixture from the food processor and test it by forming a small ball. The mix should not be too loose and should hold its form. If it is too loose, sprinkle a little gluten-free flour into the mixture and stir until well combined.

9. Use your hands to form patties about 2½ inches thick and place on the prepared baking pan.

10. Bake for 15 minutes, turning halfway through to ensure that the burgers are cooked evenly. The burgers should be firm and not wet when fully cooked.

11. Remove from the oven and serve.

Smothered Black-Eyed Pea Fritters

NUT-FREE, SOY-FREE, 30 MINUTES OR LESS

SERVES 6 TO 8 • PREP TIME: 10 MINUTES • COOK TIME: 15 MINUTES

1 cup frozen black-eyed
    peas, thawed

¼ cup unbleached
    all-purpose flour

½ teaspoon baking powder

½ teaspoon garlic powder

½ teaspoon onion powder

Pinch cayenne pepper

1 teaspoon salt

Freshly ground
    black pepper

Water

2 cups grapeseed oil

1½ cups Peach-Habanero
    Barbecue Sauce
    (page 117)

These irresistibly crunchy and crispy pea balls are traditionally from West Africa and were brought to the Americas by enslaved people. These fritters are sold as cheap street food throughout West Africa, but you can now enjoy them in the comfort of your home.

1. In a food processor, combine the peas, flour, baking powder, garlic powder, onion powder, cayenne pepper, salt, black pepper, and a few drops of water and blend until smooth and well combined.

2. Heat the oil in a saucepan over medium heat.

3. Once the oil is hot, carefully drop spoonfuls of the mix into the oil.

4. Fry until golden brown, 2 to 3 minutes on each side. Remove from the oil, drain on a paper bag, and smother with the barbecue sauce.

Jerk Barbecue Sauce, *page 119*
Mushroom Gravy, *page 120*
Tartar Sauce, *page 121*
Blackened Seasoning, *page 122*
Creole Cajun Seasoning, *page 123*

Chapter Seven

Sauces and Staples

Poppin' Southern Comeback Sauce

GLUTEN-FREE, NUT-FREE, SOY-FREE, 30 MINUTES OR LESS

MAKES 2 CUPS • PREP TIME: 5 MINUTES

1 cup vegan mayonnaise

¼ cup sweet Thai
   chile sauce

¼ cup ketchup

¼ cup sunflower oil

1 teaspoon vegan
   Worcestershire

1 teaspoon spicy
   brown mustard

1½ teaspoons
   granulated garlic

1 teaspoon onion powder

Sea salt

Freshly ground
   black pepper

This popular sauce originated in Louisiana and may remind you of a Thousand Island dressing or remoulade. The name "comeback" comes from the Louisiana people, who favored "y'all come back now" over "goodbye." The flavors of this sauce will have you coming back for more.

In a medium bowl, whisk all the ingredients until well combined. Season with salt and pepper.

Tip: Store the sauce in a sealed container in the refrigerator for 5 days. Serve as a dipping sauce for Fried Okra (page 95) or as a dressing on Crispy Fishless Po'boy Sliders (page 110).

Peach-Habanero Barbecue Sauce

GLUTEN-FREE, NUT-FREE, SOY-FREE

MAKES 2 CUPS • PREP TIME: 5 MINUTES • COOK TIME: 35 MINUTES

1 teaspoon sunflower oil

⅓ cup diced onion

2 tablespoons
    minced garlic

1 habanero pepper

1½ cups ketchup

3 tablespoons brown sugar

1½ tablespoons apple
    cider vinegar

2 tablespoons blackstrap
    molasses

1 teaspoon
    smoked paprika

⅓ cup peach juice or
    blended peaches

Pinch cayenne pepper

Some of the best barbecue sauces I've had are slow-cooked for hours to give them a richer flavor. This quick barbecue sauce achieves the same richness and flavor without taking hours. This recipe is a version of my award-winning Mango-Habanero Barbecue Sauce, but made with peaches for a southern flair.

1. In a medium saucepan, heat the oil over medium-high heat.

2. Once the oil is hot, add the onion and cook for 2 to 3 minutes or until translucent. Add the garlic and whole habanero pepper, stir, and cook for another minute.

3. Add the ketchup, brown sugar, vinegar, molasses, smoked paprika, peach juice, and cayenne pepper, and with a wooden spoon stir to mix the sauce until well combined.

4. Turn the heat to medium-low and allow to simmer for 20 to 30 minutes, or until the sauce begins to thicken and gets a little darker.

5. Remove and discard habanero pepper before serving.

Tip: This sauce pairs well with meat replacements like riblets, crispy tofu, and bean burgers. If you have the time, prepare this recipe in a slow cooker for even more depth of flavor.

Watermelon Barbecue Sauce

GLUTEN-FREE, NUT-FREE

MAKES 2 CUPS • PREP TIME: 5 MINUTES • COOK TIME: 30 MINUTES

1 teaspoon sunflower oil

¼ cup diced onion

2 or 3 garlic cloves, minced

1 cup cubed seedless
  watermelon

1 tablespoon tamari

2 teaspoons chili powder

1 teaspoon
  smoked paprika

3 tablespoons brown sugar

6 tablespoons
  tomato paste

Watermelon is not only a super-sweet fruit that has amazing health benefits, but it can also be used in many ways in the culinary world and in soul food cuisine. In this recipe I use watermelon purée to add flavor depth to barbecue sauce, which can be used as a glaze on tofu or riblets or as a dipping sauce for Crispy Avocado Fries (page 68).

1. In a medium saucepan, heat the oil over medium-high heat.

2. Once the oil is hot, add the onions and cook for 2 to 3 minutes, or until translucent. Add the garlic, stir, and cook for another minute.

3. While the onions are cooking, purée the watermelon cubes in a blender for 1 to 2 minutes.

4. Add the watermelon purée to the onions and garlic, then add the tamari, chili powder, smoked paprika, brown sugar, and tomato paste and whisk to mix well.

5. Turn the heat to medium-low and simmer for 25 minutes, or until the desired consistency is reached.

6. Allow the sauce to cool for 5 minutes before removing from the saucepan.

Tip: Store in a sealed container in the refrigerator for up to 5 days.

Jerk Barbecue Sauce

GLUTEN-FREE, NUT-FREE, SOY-FREE

MAKES 2 CUPS • PREP TIME: 5 MINUTES • COOK TIME: 35 MINUTES

1 teaspoon sunflower oil

⅓ cup diced onions

2 garlic cloves, minced

1½ cups ketchup

1 tablespoon brown sugar

¼ cup blackstrap molasses

**1 teaspoon
  smoked paprika**

**2 tablespoons Jerk
  Seasoning (page 125)**

**2 tablespoons apple
  cider vinegar**

Not only is this the top-selling sauce at my restaurant, it's also my personal favorite. The not-too-spicy jerk seasoning gives this sauce a nice flavor pop. I love to use this sauce on Crispy Cauliflower Wings (page 106) or as pizza sauce.

1. In a medium saucepan, heat the oil over medium-high heat.

2. Once the oil is hot, add the onion and cook for 2 to 3 minutes, or until translucent. Add the garlic, stir, and cook for another minute.

3. Add the ketchup, brown sugar, molasses, smoked paprika, jerk seasoning, and vinegar and whisk to mix well.

4. Turn the heat down to medium-low and simmer for 20 to 30 minutes, or until the sauce begins to thicken and gets a little darker.

Tip: To turn up the heat, add 1 teaspoon of cayenne pepper or a few dashes of your favorite hot sauce.

Mushroom Gravy

NUT-FREE, SOY-FREE, 30 MINUTES OR LESS

MAKES 4 CUPS • PREP TIME: 5 MINUTES • COOK TIME: 15 MINUTES

¼ cup sunflower oil

½ cup sliced baby
   portobello or button
   mushrooms

1 medium onion,
   thinly sliced

½ teaspoon dried thyme

Sea salt

Freshly ground
   black pepper

¼ cup unbleached
   all-purpose flour

3 to 4 cups vegetable
   stock or unsweetened
   plant-based milk

Mushrooms add a real heartiness and a nice texture to this gravy. It's terrific paired with Buttermilk Biscuits (page 132), Garlic-Smashed Potatoes (page 71), Country-Fried Mushroom Steaks (page 100), and many other dishes.

1. In a medium stockpot over medium-high heat, heat the oil, then add the mushrooms, onion, and thyme, season with salt and pepper, and stir.

2. Turn the heat down to low and cook for 5 to 7 minutes. Stir in the flour until well combined. Allow to lightly brown, then add the stock and stir.

3. Cook for 5 to 8 minutes, or until the gravy is the desired thickness.

Tartar Sauce

GLUTEN-FREE, NUT-FREE, SOY-FREE, 30 MINUTES OR LESS

MAKES 1 CUP • PREP TIME: 5 MINUTES

½ cup vegan mayonnaise

2 tablespoons sweet relish

2 teaspoons dried dill

½ teaspoon garlic powder

½ teaspoon onion powder

1 teaspoon pickle juice

1 teaspoon lemon or
   lime juice

This plant-based tartar sauce is simple and delicious. Fried fish on Fridays was a thing when I was growing up, and to be honest, I don't think my family ever used store-bought tartar sauce. We always seemed to have the ingredients on hand, so my mom or nana could always whip some up while the fish was frying. This recipe is just as quick, and I usually always have these ingredients on hand as well. Use any vegan mayonnaise you prefer, but I have found that Just Mayo and Best Foods are the thickest and taste most like traditional mayonnaise.

In a large bowl, combine all the ingredients. Whisk to blend well.

Notes: Not only can this sauce be used on or with fishless fish-inspired meals, it's also yummy on sandwiches, wraps, or bean burgers. Store in a glass jar or sealed container in the refrigerator for up to 7 days.

Blackened Seasoning

GLUTEN-FREE, NUT-FREE, OIL-FREE, SOY-FREE, 30 MINUTES OR LESS

MAKES ⅔ CUP • PREP TIME: 5 MINUTES

4 tablespoons
   smoked paprika

1 tablespoon
   cayenne pepper

2 tablespoons
   garlic powder

2 tablespoons
   onion powder

1½ teaspoons salt

1 teaspoon freshly ground
   black pepper

2 teaspoons dried thyme

2 teaspoons dried oregano

2 teaspoons dried basil

"Blackened" is sometimes mistaken as being charred. Even though I do like a nice char on my roasted vegetables, the two are quite different. Blackening involves dipping an ingredient in butter and then rubbing it with a specific blend of spices before cooking. Charring involves a light burning on the outside of an ingredient. This seasoning blend is a traditional southern recipe that brings big flavor to any dish.

Put all the ingredients in a small glass or plastic container with a lid. Seal the container and shake to mix.

Creole Cajun Seasoning

GLUTEN-FREE, NUT-FREE, OIL-FREE, SOY-FREE, 30 MINUTES OR LESS

MAKES 1⅓ CUPS • PREP TIME: 5 MINUTES

3 tablespoons
  dried oregano

2 tablespoons freshly
  ground black pepper

1 tablespoon white pepper

½ tablespoon
  cayenne pepper

3 tablespoons
  granulated garlic

2 tablespoons
  onion powder

⅓ cup smoked or
  regular paprika

3 tablespoons dried thyme

2 tablespoons dried basil

1 teaspoon salt

This amazing spice blend can be used for so many dishes that I make it weekly. Feel free to double or triple this batch if you plan on making most of the recipes in this book.

Put all the ingredients in a small glass or plastic container with a lid. Seal the container and shake to mix.

Buffalo Sauce

GLUTEN-FREE, NUT-FREE, SOY-FREE, 30 MINUTES OR LESS

MAKES 1½ CUPS • PREP TIME: 5 MINUTES

⅔ cup Frank's
RedHot sauce

½ cup sunflower oil

1 tablespoon apple
cider vinegar

¼ teaspoon vegan
Worcestershire sauce

⅓ cup maple syrup

½ tablespoon
granulated garlic

Legend has it that Frank's RedHot sauce was used to create the original buffalo wing sauce. Personally, I'm not a big fan of Frank's RedHot sauce by itself, and I don't believe in serving food I would not eat, so I created this recipe. Now I can enjoy the popular buffalo cauliflower wings I sell in my restaurant. Traditional buffalo sauces use butter, but you won't miss it in this version.

In a medium mixing bowl, whisk together all the ingredients until well combined.

Tip: This buffalo sauce is delicious with Crispy Cauliflower Wings (page 106) or as a dipping sauce for Cajun Fried "Chicken" (page 90).

Jerk Seasoning

GLUTEN-FREE, NUT-FREE, OIL-FREE, SOY-FREE, 30 MINUTES OR LESS

MAKES ½ CUP • PREP TIME: 5 MINUTES

1½ tablespoons dried thyme

2 teaspoons dried parsley

1 tablespoon brown sugar

1 teaspoon cinnamon

1 teaspoon cumin

½ teaspoon crushed red pepper flakes

1 teaspoon freshly ground black pepper

1 teaspoon allspice

2 teaspoons smoked paprika

½ teaspoon cayenne pepper

1 tablespoon onion powder

1 tablespoon granulated garlic

Traditional jerk sauce originated on the Caribbean island of Jamaica. Jerk is usually a wet spice rub used on meats that are grilled, roasted, or baked. My recipe is more of a dry rub that can be used in sauces or to coat vegetables and vegan meat substitutes. To make this into a marinade, add ⅓ cup pineapple juice and 3 tablespoons grapeseed oil and stir together. This marinade works well on tofu or cauliflower steaks or on shredded jackfruit. The combination of tangy, sweet, and spicy is truly delicious.

Put all the ingredients in a small glass or plastic container with a lid. Seal the container and shake to mix.

Tip: This jerk seasoning recipe is not as hot as some might like it, so feel free to add more cayenne pepper and crushed red pepper flakes to turn up the heat!

Cajun Chipotle Aioli

GLUTEN-FREE, NUT-FREE, SOY-FREE, 30 MINUTES OR LESS

MAKES 4 CUPS • PREP TIME: 5 MINUTES

2½ cups vegan mayonnaise

1 tablespoon lime juice

1 (20-ounce) can pineapple chunks in 100 percent juice

3 or 4 chipotles in adobo sauce

1 to 2 tablespoons adobo sauce from canned chipotles

1½ teaspoons Creole Cajun Seasoning (page 123)

2 garlic cloves, minced

½ teaspoon onion powder

Pinch white pepper

I use this sauce for more than just sandwiches. I love it as a dressing on green salads or pasta salads or as a dip for raw veggies with hummus. My favorite way to serve this aioli is on a bean burger or as a dip for Crispy Avocado Fries (page 68). It's also great on po'boy sandwiches. For the vegan mayonnaise, I prefer Just Mayo or Best Foods brands.

1. In a high-speed blender, combine all the ingredients and blend for 1 to 2 minutes.

2. Use a spatula to scrape down the sides and then blend for another minute or so.

3. Once the aioli is fully blended, pour into a glass container with a lid and use or store in the refrigerator for 7 to 10 days.

Plum-Tahini Dressing

GLUTEN-FREE, NUT-FREE, 30 MINUTES OR LESS

MAKES ⅔ CUP • PREP TIME: 5 MINUTES

¼ cup plum juice

¼ cup tahini

1½ teaspoons granulated garlic

½ tablespoon lime juice

1 tablespoon tamari

¼ teaspoon ginger

¼ cup sunflower oil

¼ teaspoon white pepper

Tahini is one of my favorite ingredients for making creamy sauces. It's made from sesame seeds, which are ground up to create a thick paste. This recipe combines the creaminess of tahini with the tangy sweetness of plums to create a vibrant dressing that is delicious on salads, bean burgers, or your favorite sandwich.

In a medium bowl, put all the ingredients and whisk together to blend.

Tip: Serve on any salad or as a dipping sauce for Zucchini and Eggplant Fries (page 72). Store refrigerated in a sealed container for up to 5 days.

Skillet Cornbread,
page 138

Breads and Biscuits

Sweet Rolls

NUT-FREE, SOY-FREE

MAKES 8 ROLLS • PREP TIME: 2 HOURS • COOK TIME: 30 MINUTES

2 tablespoons cane sugar

1 teaspoon rapid dry yeast

2½ tablespoons
    warm water

½ cup pineapple juice, plus
    more for brushing tops
    of rolls

2 tablespoons coconut
    oil, melted

1¾ cups unbleached
    all-purpose flour, plus
    more for rolling out
    the dough

These are my vegan version of Hawaiian rolls, made without butter and honey. We typically serve these rolls in my restaurant during the holidays or as slider specials.

1. In a small bowl, combine the sugar, yeast, and warm water. Stir gently and set aside for 10 minutes.

2. In another small bowl, combine ½ cup of pineapple juice and the coconut oil and stir.

3. Add the yeast mixture to the pineapple mixture and stir gently.

4. Add 1¾ cups of flour, and mix with your hands until well combined. The dough should not be too sticky. Knead in the bowl for 10 minutes, or until the dough is soft and smooth.

5. Place the dough in an oiled bowl, cover with a clean, damp towel, and place in a warm area for 1 hour to allow it to rise.

6. On a lightly floured surface, knead the dough, incorporating the flour from the surface. Break the dough into 8 equal pieces and form rolls.

7. Place the rolls on an oiled baking pan and allow to rise again for 30 to 40 minutes. Twenty minutes into this second rise, preheat the oven to 375°F.

8. Use a pastry brush to brush the tops of the rolls with pineapple juice.

9. Bake for 25 to 30 minutes or until golden brown.

Cornbread Waffles

NUT-FREE, SOY-FREE, 30 MINUTES OR LESS

SERVES 6 • PREP TIME: 10 MINUTES • COOK TIME: 5 MINUTES

⅓ cup unsweetened
    plant-based milk

1 teaspoon apple
    cider vinegar

½ teaspoon baking powder

½ teaspoon baking soda

1 cup fine cornmeal

½ cup masa

1 cup unbleached
    all-purpose flour

⅓ cup unsweetened
    applesauce

¼ cup sunflower oil

Coconut oil cooking spray

I love this recipe because not only is it easy, it's a super creative and tasty way to transform traditional southern cornbread into a truly wow-worthy dish. Serve with Caribbean Coconut Greens (page 62), Candied Yams (page 70), and Jerk Barbecue-Pulled Mushrooms (page 99) for a perfect southern meal.

1. In a small bowl, whisk together the milk and vinegar and set aside.

2. In another small bowl, whisk the baking powder, baking soda, cornmeal, masa, and flour together.

3. Add the applesauce and oil to the bowl containing the milk and stir to mix.

4. Pour the wet ingredients into the dry ingredients and whisk until well combined.

5. Turn a waffle iron on and coat with cooking spray.

6. When the iron is hot, pour in enough batter to fill the waffle iron and cook for 4 to 5 minutes, or until lightly golden brown.

7. Take the waffle out of the waffle iron and cut it in half. Repeat with the remaining batter

Buttermilk Biscuits

NUT-FREE, 30 MINUTES OR LESS

MAKES 8 BISCUITS • PREP TIME: 15 MINUTES • COOK TIME: 15 MINUTES

1 cup plant-based milk

1 tablespoon apple
cider vinegar

2 cups unbleached
all-purpose flour, plus
more for cutting out
the biscuits

1 tablespoon
baking powder

½ teaspoon baking soda

½ teaspoon salt

1 tablespoon cane sugar

4 tablespoons (½ stick)
Earth Balance vegan
butter, cold

These biscuits take me back in time, when Nana would whip up the most amazing, fluffy, buttery, melt-in-your-mouth biscuits in just minutes.

1. Preheat the oven to 450°F and line a baking pan with parchment paper.

2. In a small bowl, mix the milk and vinegar and allow to curdle, usually no more than 5 minutes.

3. In a medium mixing bowl, whisk together the flour, baking powder, baking soda, salt, and sugar.

4. Add the cold butter and use your fingers or a pastry cutter to combine until only small pieces remain and the mixture looks grainy, like sand. Work fast so the butter doesn't get too soft.

5. Make a well in the dry ingredients, and use a wooden spoon to stir gently while pouring in the milk mixture ¼ cup at a time. Stir until well combined.

6. Sprinkle flour on a clean surface and dump the dough onto it. Dust the top of the dough with flour. Gently flatten the dough with your hands until it is about 1 inch thick, then dip a coffee mug rim into the flour to coat it and use it to cut out the biscuits.

7. Place the cut biscuits on the lined baking pan, and bake for 6 minutes, then turn and bake another 6 minutes or until the tops and edges turn golden brown.

....

Tip: Store the biscuits in a sealed container in the refrigerator for up to 3 days or freeze for up to 30 days. After you combine the ingredients, the dough might be looser than traditional biscuit dough. This is typical; just be sure to flour your surface, your hands, and the mug rim before cutting out the biscuits.

Gluten-Free Biscuits

GLUTEN-FREE, 30 MINUTES OR LESS

SERVES 6 • PREP TIME: 10 MINUTES • COOKING TIME: 15 MINUTES

1 cup unsweetened
   almond milk
1 tablespoon apple
   cider vinegar
3 cups gluten-free baking
   flour (I prefer Bob's
   Red Mill)
1 tablespoon
   baking powder
½ teaspoon baking soda
2 pinches sea salt
4 tablespoons (½ stick)
   Earth Balance vegan
   butter, cold

These gluten-free biscuits are fluffy and will certainly fulfill that buttery biscuit craving. Since more than half of my clientele has some form of gluten allergies, I make it a priority to create gluten-free versions of almost anything I make. I prefer to use Bob's Red Mill Gluten-Free 1-to-1 Baking Flour. I have tried many other brands, including making my own blend, and found that often the recipes come out grainy or just plain hard, but Bob's blend is wonderful and keeps dishes moist without a super-grainy taste.

1. Preheat the oven to 400°F.

2. In a small mixing bowl, combine the milk and vinegar and stir. Set aside for 5 to 10 minutes.

3. In a medium mixing bowl, whisk together the flour, baking powder, baking soda, and salt.

4. Cut in the cold butter, then add the wet ingredients and stir gently with a wooden spoon or your hands until well combined. Be careful not to overmix, or the biscuits will become hard.

5. On a lightly floured surface, turn out the dough and flatten slightly with your hands. Use a biscuit cutter or the lid of a large mason jar to cut out the biscuits.

6. Place the biscuits on an oiled baking pan.

7. Bake for 15 minutes, or until lightly browned on top.

Pie Dough

NUT-FREE

MAKES 2 (9-INCH) PIE CRUSTS • PREP TIME: 15 MINUTES, PLUS 1 HOUR TO REFRIGERATE DOUGH • COOK TIME: 5 MINUTES

1¼ cups unbleached all-purpose flour
¼ teaspoon sea salt
8 tablespoons (1 stick) Earth Balance vegan butter, cold
¼ cup ice water

This pie crust is not only easy to make, but it's flaky, buttery, and delicious! The dough can be premade and rolled out a day or so ahead. To store, just roll out the dough and then gently fold, wrap with plastic wrap, and place in the refrigerator or freezer until ready to use. I prefer to use Earth Balance vegan butter over most others because of the buttery flavor and the balance of water. Many other vegan butters contain more water.

1. In a large bowl, combine the flour and salt and stir to mix well.

2. Cut the cold butter into the flour and mix with your hands until the mixture resembles crumbs.

3. Stir in the ice water a little at a time.

4. Form two equally sized balls with the dough, wrap in plastic wrap, and then refrigerate for 1 hour or overnight.

5. Remove one ball of dough from the refrigerator and unwrap. On a lightly floured surface, roll out the dough to fit a 9-inch pie pan. Fit into the pan, and use a fork to poke holes in the bottom of the pie dough. Parbake for 5 minutes. (Parbaking is cooking something until it's slightly underdone.)

6. The crust is now ready to be filled with your favorite pie filling and baked. Roll out the second ball of dough to top your pie, or refrigerate for up to 3 days.

Yeast Rolls

NUT-FREE

MAKES 12 ROLLS • PREP TIME: 2 HOURS • COOK TIME: 20 MINUTES

4½ cups unbleached all-purpose flour, plus more for kneading and rolling out the dough

½ teaspoon sea salt

1 teaspoon rapid-rising instant yeast

2 tablespoons coconut sugar

8 tablespoons (1 stick) Earth Balance vegan butter, melted, plus more to brush on top of rolls

1 cup unsweetened oat milk

½ cup water

Oh, the smell of yeast rolls takes me back to my childhood, as these rolls were my nana's favorite. I swear we'd have at least four dozen yeast rolls at every Sunday dinner as well as on special occasions. I remember wishing those rolls would hurry up and rise the second time, because I knew I'd be able to eat one as soon as it came out of the oven. My recipe replaces white sugar with coconut sugar and uses vegan butter and oat milk.

1. Preheat the oven to 350°F.

2. In a large bowl, combine the flour, salt, yeast, and sugar and whisk to stir well.

3. In a medium bowl, combine the melted butter, oat milk, and water and stir.

4. Make a well in the dry ingredients, then pour the wet mix in and mix with a wooden spoon or your hands until all the ingredients are incorporated.

5. Knead the dough for 8 minutes or until smooth. If the dough is too sticky, add a bit more flour and knead a little longer.

6. Place the dough in an oiled bowl, cover with plastic wrap or a clean, damp towel, and allow to rise for 45 minutes.

7. Once the dough has risen, turn it out on a lightly floured surface, then roll it out to make 12 rolls.

8. Place the rolls on an oiled baking pan. Cover and allow to rise for another 45 minutes.

9. Uncover the rolls, brush the tops with melted vegan butter, and bake for 20 minutes or until golden brown on top.

....

Tip: These rolls make delicious slider buns if you have any left over. Store in a zip-top bag for 3 days. Use any leftover rolls for bread pudding.

Skillet Cornbread

NUT-FREE, SOY-FREE

SERVES 10 • PREP TIME: 10 MINUTES • COOK TIME: 30 MINUTES

1 (13.5-ounce) can
   coconut milk
1 teaspoon apple
   cider vinegar
1 cup cornmeal
1 cup unbleached
   all-purpose flour
²/₃ cup unsweetened
   applesauce
½ cup coconut sugar
¼ cup coconut oil, melted
1 tablespoon
   baking powder
2 pinches sea salt

I don't know anyone who doesn't love cornbread. This was actually something I thought I wouldn't be able to have after transitioning to a vegan diet. Who knew there were so many wonderful egg replacements that can add even more dimension to your recipes? Here applesauce is used as the egg replacement, and it gives an extraordinary moistness to the bread.

1. Preheat the oven to 350°F.

2. In a measuring cup or small mixing bowl, combine the milk and vinegar, stir, and set aside.

3. In a large bowl, combine the cornmeal, flour, applesauce, sugar, oil, baking powder, and salt and stir with a wooden spoon to combine.

4. Add the milk mixture and mix well.

5. Into a cast-iron skillet or oiled baking pan, pour the cornbread mixture and gently flatten with a wooden spoon.

6. Bake for 30 minutes or until the top is golden brown and the center is firm.

7. Take out of the oven and allow to cool for 5 minutes and serve.

Tip: Add ½ cup corn kernels, ½ cup vegan shredded cheddar, and 1 diced jalapeño to add more bite and southern flair to this delicious cornbread.

Southern Pecan Bread

SOY-FREE

SERVES 6 TO 8 • PREP TIME: 5 MINUTES • COOKING TIME: 30 MINUTES

¾ cup unsweetened
   applesauce
½ cup cane sugar
¾ cup brown sugar
1 cup sunflower oil
1 teaspoon vanilla extract
½ teaspoon cinnamon
1 cup self-rising flour
2 cups chopped pecans

This southern classic is a terrific way to enjoy pecans. If you don't have pecans on hand, feel free to swap out the nuts and even add pumpkin seeds. This bread is best mixed with a wooden spoon instead of a hand mixer, as it's important not to overmix it. Overmixing can create too much gluten in the flour and cause the bread to become hard. Enjoy this bread as a snack or a dessert or with your morning tea or coffee.

1. Preheat the oven to 350°F.

2. In a large bowl, combine the applesauce, cane sugar, brown sugar, oil, vanilla, and cinnamon and stir well.

3. Add the flour and pecans and stir to combine.

4. Pour the mixture into an oiled 9-by-13-inch baking dish and gently level.

5. Bake for 30 minutes or until a toothpick inserted in the center comes out clean.

Pecan Pie
Mini Tarts,
page 151

Chapter Nine

Desserts

Coconut Bread Pudding

NUT-FREE, SOY-FREE

SERVES 4 • PREP TIME: 20 MINUTES • COOK TIME: 30 MINUTES

2 cups cubed bread

1 (13-ounce) can coconut milk

¾ cup coconut sugar

⅓ cup coconut oil, melted

1 teaspoon vanilla extract

½ teaspoon cinnamon

¼ cup raisins

⅓ cup unsweetened shredded coconut

Nonstick cooking spray

My mother made the best bread pudding. Growing up, I can remember seeing a big bowl of soaking bread cubes that smelled so fragrant, I could have tried a piece of bread right out of the bowl. I must admit that my version still is not as good as my mother's, but I think you'll be quite pleased with it.

1. Preheat the oven to 350°F.

2. Place the bread cubes in a large mixing bowl.

3. In a medium mixing bowl, combine the milk, sugar, oil, vanilla, and cinnamon and whisk together.

4. Add the raisins and the coconut shreds to the bowl containing the cubed bread, then pour the milk mixture over the bread and gently toss, making sure all the bread pieces are covered.

5. Allow to sit for 15 minutes, until the bread soaks up most of the liquid.

6. Pour the bread mixture into four individual ramekins coated with nonstick cooking spray.

7. Place the ramekins on a baking pan.

8. Bake for 25 to 30 minutes.

9. Remove from the oven and allow to cool for 5 minutes, then serve.

Butternut Squash Pie

NUT-FREE, SOY-FREE

SERVES 8 • PREP TIME: 10 MINUTES • COOK TIME: 1 HOUR

Nonstick cooking spray

2 cups cubed butternut squash

Oil, for drizzling

2 tablespoons flax meal

⅓ cup water

⅓ cup agave nectar or maple syrup

1 teaspoon cinnamon

½ teaspoon powdered ginger

½ cup coconut oil

1 cup coconut milk

1 tablespoon unbleached all-purpose flour

1 9-inch pie crust, parbaked (see page 135)

I had no idea how delicious butternut squash could be until years ago when a baker friend of mine made me try his pie. It was instantly a favorite, and I quickly got to work creating my own. I prefer this pie over sweet potato, pumpkin, or bean pies. If I don't bring this pie to every family gathering, my pop-pop might not speak to me. I even make Pop-pop his own squash pie for Thanksgiving, he loves it so much!

1. Preheat the oven to 420°F. Line a baking pan with parchment paper or spray with nonstick cooking spray.

2. Place the squash on the prepared baking pan, drizzle with oil, and lightly toss to ensure that all sides of the squash are coated. Bake for 12 to 15 minutes, or until the squash is fork-tender.

3. While the squash is roasting, in a small bowl or cup, combine the flax meal and water and set aside for 10 minutes.

4. Remove the butternut squash from the oven.

5. In a blender, combine the agave nectar, cinnamon, ginger, oil, milk, flour, flax mixture, and squash and blend well.

6. Pour the mixture into the parbaked pie crust and use a baking spatula to smooth out the top.

Continued

Butternut Squash Pie *Continued*

7. Bake for 40 to 45 minutes, or until the pie is firm and lightly browned on the edges and begins to show cracks.

8. Remove from the oven and allow to cool for 10 minutes, then slice and serve.

....

Tip: Take this pie to another level by adding vegan cream cheese swirls. Blend 1 (8-ounce) package of vegan cream cheese (I prefer Trader Joe's brand) with 1½ tablespoons of powdered sugar, then add dollops around the pie and use a butter knife to make lines that swirl left to right in the cream cheese dollops before baking.

Berry Cobbler

SERVES 6 · PREP TIME: 15 MINUTES · COOK TIME: 30 MINUTES

20 ounces frozen
mixed berries

½ cup cane sugar

1 tablespoon cornstarch

1 teaspoon lemon or
lime juice

¾ cup unbleached
all-purpose flour

¾ teaspoon baking powder

Pinch salt

4 tablespoons (½ stick)
Earth Balance
vegan butter

2 tablespoons
unsweetened
almond milk

Cobblers are a staple in soul food and southern cuisine. Berries, especially blackberries, grow abundantly in the South, and this is a perfect way to utilize the fruit. Berry cobbler is my youngest son's favorite, so I could probably make this recipe with my eyes closed, I've made it so many times over the years.

1. Preheat the oven to 375°F.

2. In a large bowl, combine the berries, sugar, cornstarch, and citrus juice and stir. Set aside.

3. In another bowl, combine the flour, baking powder, and salt and stir. Fold in the butter and crumble with your hands. Slowly add the milk and mix gently.

4. Pour the berry mixture into an oiled cast-iron skillet or a coated baking dish.

5. Use a large spoon to gently drop spoonfuls of the flour mixture on top of the berries, making sure the dough drops are not too far apart.

6. Bake for 30 minutes, or until the sides are bubbling and the dough is browned. Allow to cool for 10 minutes before serving.

Avocado Mousse

GLUTEN-FREE, NUT-FREE, OIL-FREE, SOY-FREE, 30 MINUTES OR LESS

SERVES 4 • PREP TIME: 5 MINUTES

2 large ripe avocados

½ cup 100 percent cocoa powder

¼ cup unsweetened plant-based milk

1 teaspoon vanilla extract

½ cup vegan chocolate chips, melted

Pinch salt

3 to 4 tablespoons agave nectar

Fruit, granola, or peanut butter, for serving

This healthy version of pudding is surprisingly yummy. I like to use avocados that are a little too soft, as they create such a creaminess in this recipe. This mousse is a great way to enjoy something sweet without eating any refined sugar and while obtaining healthy fats along the way.

1. In a high-speed blender, combine all the ingredients (except the topping for serving) and blend until well incorporated.

2. Use a spatula to remove the mousse from the blender.

3. Serve in parfait cups topped with fruit, granola, or peanut butter.

Tip: Store the mousse in an airtight container in the refrigerator for up to 3 days.

Cranberry Crumble

NUT-FREE

SERVES 6 • PREP TIME: 10 MINUTES • COOK TIME: 30 MINUTES

Oil or nonstick cooking spray

FOR THE FILLING

1 cup fresh cranberries
¼ cup coconut sugar
1 tablespoon lemon or lime juice
2 tablespoons agave nectar or maple syrup
1 tablespoon cornstarch

FOR THE TOPPING

1 cup unbleached all-purpose flour
½ cup quick-cooking oats
¼ cup coconut sugar
Pinch sea salt
1 teaspoon baking powder
8 tablespoons (1 stick) Earth Balance vegan butter
1 tablespoon coconut milk

This recipe combines sweet and tart to create these individual crumble pies. It's easy, quick, and a healthier version that omits refined sugar and regular butter while not compromising on taste. Get your taste buds ready for this treat!

1. Preheat the oven to 375°F. Prepare six individual ramekins by coating them with oil or cooking spray.

2. To make the filling, in a medium bowl, combine the cranberries, sugar, citrus juice, agave nectar, and cornstarch and stir well. Set aside.

3. To make the topping, in another medium bowl, combine the flour, oats, sugar, salt, and baking powder and whisk together. Add the butter and milk, then mix with a fork until well combined.

4. Fill the ramekins: Spoon a small amount of the flour mixture into each ramekin and press into the bottom, then fill ¾ full with cranberries and top with a large spoonful of the flour mixture.

5. Place the filled ramekins on a baking pan.

6. Bake for 25 to 30 minutes or until the cranberries are bubbling and the crumble topping has browned.

Peach Cobbler

NUT-FREE

SERVES 6 • PREP TIME: 10 MINUTES • COOK TIME: 40 MINUTES

FOR THE FILLING

3 cups sliced peaches

¼ cup cane sugar

1 tablespoon cornstarch

1 teaspoon vanilla extract

½ teaspoon ground
   cinnamon

FOR THE TOPPING

1 cup unbleached
   all-purpose flour

1 teaspoon baking powder

Pinch salt

8 tablespoons (1 stick)
   Earth Balance
   vegan butter

2 tablespoons
   unsweetened
   plant-based milk

Georgia is known for its amazingly sweet peaches, and to be honest, when I lived there, I made the absolute best cobblers I've ever had. There's something magical about Georgia's peaches. This recipe is my oldest son's favorite, so I put extra love into it each time I make it.

1. Preheat the oven to 375°F.

2. To make the filling, in a large bowl, combine the peaches, sugar, cornstarch, vanilla, and cinnamon and stir well.

3. To make the topping, in another large bowl, combine the flour, baking powder, and salt and stir to combine. Fold in the butter and crumble with your hands. Slowly add the milk and mix gently.

4. Pour the peach mixture into a greased 8-by-8-inch baking dish.

5. Use a large spoon to gently drop spoonfuls of the flour mixture on top of the peaches, making sure the dough drops are not too far apart.

6. Bake for 30 to 40 minutes, or until the sides are bubbling and the topping is browned.

Caramel-Apple Cheesecake Bars

NUT-FREE

MAKES 9 BARS • PREP TIME: 15 MINUTES, PLUS 1 HOUR TO SET • COOK TIME: 45 MINUTES

FOR THE CRUST

2 cups unbleached
    all-purpose flour
½ cup coconut sugar
1 cup (2 sticks) Earth
    Balance vegan butter

FOR THE FILLING

2 (8-ounce) packages
    vegan cream cheese
1 teaspoon vanilla extract
4 tablespoons
    aquafaba, whipped
½ cup plus 2 tablespoons
    cane sugar, divided
3 Granny Smith apples,
    peeled, cored, and diced
½ teaspoon ground
    cinnamon

FOR THE TOPPING

1 cup unbleached
    all-purpose flour
½ cup quick-cooking oats
8 tablespoons (1 stick)
    Earth Balance vegan
    butter, at room
    temperature
½ cup coconut sugar or
    brown sugar

I usually make this recipe for the holidays. We started making these bars last year at my restaurant and couldn't keep up with the demand. They are wonderful for any occasion and work especially well as party desserts cut into bite-size pieces. For the cream cheese, I prefer Trader Joe's brand or Tofutti.

1. Preheat the oven to 350°F. Prepare a 9-by-9-inch baking dish by lining it with parchment paper or coating it with cooking spray.

2. In a medium bowl, combine the crust ingredients and mix with a fork or pastry cutter until crumbly.

3. Press the crust evenly into the prepared baking dish and bake until lightly browned, about 15 minutes.

4. In a medium bowl, combine the cream cheese, vanilla, aquafaba, and ½ cup of cane sugar and mix with a hand mixer.

5. In another medium bowl, combine the apples, the remaining 2 tablespoons of cane sugar, and the cinnamon and stir to mix well.

6. In a small bowl, combine the topping ingredients and mix with your hands until crumbly.

7. Pour the cream cheese mixture over the warm crust, then top with the apple mixture. Sprinkle the crumbled topping evenly over the apples and bake for about 30 minutes.

Continued

Caramel-Apple Cheesecake Bars *Continued*

FOR THE CARAMEL

1 cup brown sugar

4 tablespoons full-fat coconut milk

8 tablespoons (1 stick) Earth Balance vegan butter

1 teaspoon vanilla extract

Pinch salt

8. While the bars are baking, combine the caramel ingredients in a saucepan and heat over medium heat until the sauce takes on a smooth, thick consistency. Remove from the heat and allow to cool.

9. Remove the bars from the oven and place in the refrigerator to cool. Allow the cheesecake to set for 1 hour or overnight.

10. Cut into 3-by-3-inch bars, drizzle with caramel, and serve.

Tip: Store in a sealed container in the refrigerator for 3 to 5 days.

Pecan Pie Mini Tarts

SERVES 12 • PREP TIME: 15 MINUTES • COOK TIME: 25 MINUTES

½ recipe Pie Dough,
    unbaked (page 135)
1 tablespoon flax meal
6 tablespoons warm water
2 tablespoons coconut oil
Pinch salt
½ cup agave nectar
½ cup maple syrup
2 cups chopped pecans
1 teaspoon vanilla extract

My fondest memory of pecan pie is from some years ago at a family reunion in North Carolina, when my sister and I went to Waffle House. After our meal, we decided to share a slice of pecan pie. The waitress asked if we wanted the "southern special." Not knowing what it was but excited to try it, we said yes. She brought us the pie, and when I tasted it, I thought it was the best thing ever! Turns out the "southern special" was pouring hot butter over the slice of pie and serving it with a scoop of vanilla ice cream. My recipe is wonderfully delicious, without all the heart-clogging unhealthy ingredients.

1. Preheat the oven to 350°F.

2. Roll out the pie dough and use the lid of a small mason jar to cut out circles of dough. Press one circle into each well of a muffin tin to form the base and sides for the tarts.

3. In a small bowl, combine the flax meal and the warm water, stir, and set aside for 5 minutes.

4. In a small saucepan, combine the coconut oil, salt, agave nectar, maple syrup, and flax mixture, bring to a soft boil, stir in the pecans and vanilla, and remove from the heat.

5. Pour the pecan mixture into the muffin tins to about half an inch below the crust line.

6. Bake for 25 minutes or until the tarts begin to bubble and the crust is golden brown.

Tip: Serve with a small scoop of plant-based ice cream or a dollop of vegan whipped cream.

Sweet Potato Hand Pies

NUT-FREE, 30 MINUTES OR LESS

SERVES 6 • PREP TIME: 10 MINUTES • COOK TIME: 20 MINUTES

Nonstick cooking spray

1 cup roasted, mashed
    sweet potato

2 tablespoons maple syrup

1 tablespoon coconut oil

1 teaspoon vanilla extract

1 teaspoon ground
    cinnamon

¼ teaspoon ground ginger

1 recipe Pie Dough,
    unbaked (page 135)

2 tablespoons Earth
    Balance vegan
    butter, melted

Sweet potato pie is traditionally served in most African American homes on holidays or special occasions. Here's a no-refined-sugar recipe that gives you perfect individual pies, so no one has to share.

1. Preheat the oven to 350°F. Prepare a baking pan by lining it with parchment or coating it with cooking spray.

2. In a blender or food processor, combine the sweet potato, maple syrup, coconut oil, vanilla, cinnamon, and ginger and blend until well combined.

3. On a lightly floured surface, roll out the dough and use the lid of a small mason jar to cut out 12 circles.

4. Lay out six dough circles on the prepared baking pan, then place 3 tablespoons of the sweet potato mixture in the middle of each circle. Place the remaining six dough circles on top of the filled circles, and use a fork to create a seal around the edges.

5. Use a pastry brush to brush the top of each hand pie with the melted butter.

6. Bake for 20 minutes or until the pies are golden brown.

Rice Pudding

GLUTEN-FREE, NUT-FREE

SERVES 6 • PREP TIME: 5 MINUTES • COOK TIME: 30 MINUTES

1 (15-ounce) can
   coconut milk
1 cup brown basmati rice,
   rinsed well
¼ cup maple syrup
2 teaspoons vanilla extract
1½ teaspoons ground
   cinnamon
1 cup raisins or dried
   cranberries
1 tablespoon Earth
   Balance vegan butter
1 cup unsweetened
   plant-based milk

I refused to eat rice pudding for years, as this was another dish my father made for us constantly one summer when it seemed like all we had to eat was different versions of beans and rice. I thought I would never eat it again, but I guess I just took a break, because now I love this dish and I'm sure you will too.

1. In a medium pot, combine the coconut milk, rice, maple syrup, vanilla, cinnamon, raisins, and butter and bring to a boil over medium heat.

2. Reduce the heat and simmer for 10 to 15 minutes, stirring occasionally to make sure the rice doesn't stick to the bottom of the pot.

3. When most of the liquid has absorbed, add the milk and stir.

4. Simmer until the pudding takes on a nice, thick consistency.

5. Remove from the heat, allow to cool for a few minutes, and then serve.

Tip: Serve topped with fresh strawberries and blueberries or shredded coconut.

Measurement Conversions

VOLUME EQUIVALENTS (LIQUID)

US STANDARD	US STANDARD (OUNCES)	METRIC (APPROXIMATE)
2 tablespoons	1 fl. oz.	30 mL
¼ cup	2 fl. oz.	60 mL
½ cup	4 fl. oz.	120 mL
1 cup	8 fl. oz.	240 mL
1½ cups	12 fl. oz.	355 mL
2 cups or 1 pint	16 fl. oz.	475 mL
4 cups or 1 quart	32 fl. oz.	1 L
1 gallon	128 fl. oz.	4 L

OVEN TEMPERATURES

FAHRENHEIT	CELSIUS (APPROXIMATE)
250°F	120°C
300°F	150°C
325°F	165°C
350°F	180°C
375°F	190°C
400°F	200°C
425°F	220°C
450°F	230°C

VOLUME EQUIVALENTS (DRY)

US STANDARD	METRIC (APPROXIMATE)
⅛ teaspoon	0.5 mL
¼ teaspoon	1 mL
½ teaspoon	2 mL
¾ teaspoon	4 mL
1 teaspoon	5 mL
1 tablespoon	15 mL
¼ cup	59 mL
⅓ cup	79 mL
½ cup	118 mL
⅔ cup	156 mL
¾ cup	177 mL
1 cup	235 mL
2 cups or 1 pint	475 mL
3 cups	700 mL
4 cups or 1 quart	1 L

WEIGHT EQUIVALENTS

US STANDARD	METRIC (APPROXIMATE)
½ ounce	15 g
1 ounce	30 g
2 ounces	60 g
4 ounces	115 g
8 ounces	225 g
12 ounces	340 g
16 ounces or 1 pound	455 g

Resources/References

American Heart Association News. "Vegan Diet May Decrease Heart Disease, Stroke Risk in African Americans." American Heart Association. December 3, 2019. heart.org/en/news/2019/12/03/vegan-diet-may-decrease-heartdisease-stroke-risk-in-african-americans.

Lardieri, Alexa. "Study: Southern Diet Contributes to Premature African-American Deaths." *U.S. News & World Report*. October 2, 2018. usnews.com/news/health-care-news/articles/2018-10-02/study-southern-diet-contributes-to-premature-african-american-deaths.

Shankman, Sabrina. "What Is Nitrous Oxide and Why Is It a Climate Threat?" *Inside Climate News*. September 11, 2019. insideclimatenews.org/news/11092019/nitrous-oxide-climate-pollutant-explainer-greenhouse-gas-agriculture-livestock.

Thornton, Alex. "This Is How Many Animals We Eat Each Year." World Economic Forum. February 8, 2019. weforum.org/agenda/2019/02/chart-of-the-day-this-is-how-many-animals-we-eat-each-year.

Tuso, Philip J., Mohamed H. Ismail, Benjamin P. Ha, and Carole Bartolotto. "Nutritional Update for Physicians: Plant-Based Diets." *Permanente Journal* 17, no. 2 (Spring 2013): 61–66. doi.org/10.7812/TPP/12-085.

UN Environment Programme. "Tackling the World's Most Urgent Problem: Meat." September 26, 2018. unenvironment.org/news-and-stories/story/tackling-worlds-most-urgent-problem-meat.

UN News. "Rearing Cattle Produces More Greenhouse Gases Than Driving Cars, UN Report Warns." November 29, 2006. news.un.org/en/story/2006/11/201222-rearing-cattle-produces-more-greenhouse-gases-driving-cars-un-report-warns.

Index

Acknowledgments

To my dad, who was the first person to plant the seeds of creating cookbooks for the people. I thank you for feeding me spiritually over the years, but especially during this process. Without you, none of this would have been possible. I am eternally grateful for your love and light!

To my youngest son, Ziare, I thank you for choosing to be by my side and holding the kitchen down while I focused on this book. Your loyalty, love, and dedication mean the world to me.

To my sister, friend, and business partner, Sabrina. Thank you for joining me on this journey. From first meeting you, who knew what was written in the stars for us? Thank you for trusting in our journey and yourself!

Lastly, to my sister Malika, our conversations are inspiration to my soul. Thank you for just being the love and light you are to me and the world!

About the Author

Nadira Jenkins-El is a vegan chef. She studied culinary management at the Art Institutes in Washington. Later, dealing with her own medical issues and wanting to heal herself holistically, Nadira chose to further her studies at the Southwest Institute of Healing Arts (SWIHA) in Tempe, Arizona, becoming a certified holistic wellness practitioner and holistic nutritionist. With a dream of creating and serving healthier alternatives, Nadira founded Global Fusion, LLC, in 2014 as a home-based vegan and gluten-free bakery and confectionary in Tucson, Arizona.

Nadira later became partners with her friend Sabrina Metherell, a pastry chef who shared the love, vision, and passion of Global Fusion. Through travel, Nadira has experienced many different kinds of cuisine firsthand, including Italian, soul food, Caribbean, Japanese, and more. After returning from her travels, she knew she had to share her gift with the world.

Global Fusion soon found a home at Zen Nights Block Party in Mesa, Arizona. Just short of the one-year anniversary of joining the Block Party, Nadira and Sabrina purchased the Cutting Board Bakery and Café in East Mesa.

Nadira won the Judge's and People Choice Awards for her mango-habanero barbecue sauce at the Zen Nights Inc and Vegan OutReach of Los Angeles's 2018 BBQ Contest. She also won the People's Choice Award for her vegan fried "chicken" at the Zen Nights Inc and Vegan Outreach of Los Angeles's 2019 Fried Chick'in Throw-down.